MW00597537

Praise for *Trust-Based Observations*

"In any field, practitioners need honest, well-intentioned, and trustworthy feedback in order to succeed and improve. If the feedback process is compromised by suspicion and anxiety, it quickly becomes useless, even counterproductive. In this thoughtful and empathetic book, Craig Randall details how teacher observation has gone awry and how to put it back on track. He offers a sensible, empirically grounded technique, as well as indispensable advice on how to build trusting relationships among educators."—Ulrich Boser, author of *Learn Better* and *The Leap: The Science of Trust and Why It Matters*

"*Trust-Based Observations* is an overdue rethink of how to support the most important asset in schools and in the lives of students: their teachers. This book honors the art and science of teaching and the complexity of creating learning environments where all students can find success and challenge."— Glenn Whitman, director of the Center for Transformative Teaching and Learning and author of *Neuroteach: Brain Science and the Future of Education*

"Most teachers view administrator observations as inauthentic for capturing what happens in classroom instruction. Most administrators want the observation process to be supportive and not an obligatory hoop to jump through. Craig Randall's book is a game changer. Honed by deep experiences, *Trust-Based Observations* combines empathy and a growth mindset to create a powerful system for professional collaboration that enables teacher growth and an empowered professional community. This book opens a new and liberating world for positive and productive classroom visits."—John McCarthy, author of *So All Can Learn*

"*Trust-Based Observations* should be on the shelf of every administrator. It offers brisk, engaging writing and makes a compelling case for why we should radically rethink teacher observations. The book is never preachy and is full of practical resources that principals and school leaders can use immediately. I have experienced Craig's trust-based method personally when he was my principal and can honestly say that the observation process was empowering, greatly impacting my subsequent work as a coach. This is a must-have for leaders that want to improve morale, feedback, and trust."—

Alexis Wiggins, director of Cohort of Educators for Essential Learning and author of *The Best Class You Never Taught*

"Written from the perspective of an educator who has a wealth of experience working in educational institutions internationally, this book provides an interesting contribution to the thinking and practice surrounding the use of observation in educational contexts. In *Trust-Based Observations*, Randall puts forward a compelling case for engaging with observation as a supportive tool for teacher learning and provides a framework for educators to apply this."—Matthew O'Leary, author of *Classroom Observation: A Guide to the Effective Observation of Teaching and Learning* and *Reclaiming Lesson Observation: Supporting Excellence in Teacher Learning*

Trust-Based Observations

Trust-Based Observations

*Maximizing Teaching
and Learning Growth*

Craig Randall

ROWMAN & LITTLEFIELD
Lanham • Boulder • New York • London

Published by Rowman & Littlefield
An imprint of The Rowman & Littlefield Publishing Group, Inc.
4501 Forbes Boulevard, Suite 200, Lanham, Maryland 20706
www.rowman.com

6 Tinworth Street, London SE11 5AL, United Kingdom

Copyright © 2020 by Craig Randall

All rights reserved. No part of this book may be reproduced in any form or by any
electronic or mechanical means, including information storage and retrieval systems,
without written permission from the publisher, except by a reviewer who may quote
passages in a review.

British Library Cataloguing in Publication Information Available

Library of Congress Cataloging-in-Publication Data

Names: Randall, Craig, 1965– author.
Title: Trust-based observations : maximizing teaching and learning growth / Craig Randall.
Description: Lanham : Rowman & Littlefield, [2020] | Includes bibliographical refer-
ences. | Summary: "Trust-Based Observations teaches observers to build trusting relation-
ships with teachers as they engage in frequent observations and reflective conversations
with them. Using the manageable observation form and data driven goal setting, the result
is teachers embrace risk-taking and take growth steps necessary for significant teaching
improvement"— Provided by publisher.
Identifiers: LCCN 2020000884 (print) | LCCN 2020000885 (ebook) | ISBN
9781475853551 (cloth) | ISBN 9781475853568 (paperback) | ISBN 9781475853575
(epub)
Subjects: LCSH: Observation (Educational method) | Teachers—Rating of. | Teachers—
Training of. | Teacher effectiveness. | Effective teaching. | Reflective teaching. | Trust.
Classification: LCC LB1027.28 .R36 2020 (print) | LCC LB1027.28 (ebook) | DDC
370.71/1—dc23
LC record available at https://lccn.loc.gov/2020000884
LC ebook record available at https://lccn.loc.gov/2020000885

♾ ™ The paper used in this publication meets the minimum requirements of American
National Standard for Information Sciences Permanence of Paper for Printed Library
Materials, ANSI/NISO Z39.48-1992.

To Warren for the idea and inspiration,
Dave for the freedom, support, and encouragement,
and Michele for her unwavering support.

Contents

Acknowledgments

First and foremost, I want to thank all the amazing teachers I have had the opportunity to work alongside. I owe you all for teaching me what the elements of great teaching are. Thank you for a gift I can never fully repay. As the saying goes (and it is true), I have learned so much more from you than I can ever give back. Your gifts are priceless to me.

The truth is that had I not come across Warren Aller, the director of my principal certification program, *Trust-Based Observations* would never have materialized. Warren opened my eyes to a new and better way of conducting observations—one about reflection, care, and growth. The foundation you provided me is still the core of TBO. Thank you.

While I was working on obtaining my principal certification, so was my friend Scott Schaffner. Our regular and lengthy talks about what does and doesn't make for a good principal and leader helped further etch the beliefs that led to *Trust-Based Observations*. Thanks, Scott.

I was lucky to be hired by Dave Christenbury, who not only gave me the freedom to pursue a new way of doing observations but also encouraged me to keep developing ideas and even adapted the model himself. I am so thankful for your mentorship, Dave.

I thank Brian Matthews for hiring me for my first principal job and allowing me the freedom to conduct my observations. I thank Nancy Jenkins for engaging in and embracing what has become *Trust-Based Observations* in her role as assistant principal. I thank Kathy Minor for forcing my hand into creating an observation form. Thanks to Donald Caldwell, Derek Lea, and Peter Thorpe for helping to create the form and practicing the observations together. I learned much from you all.

Thank you to Michael Boots for allowing and encouraging me to teach TBO to the other principals I worked with. Thank you to Bryan Bibby-Smith for being the first to recognize that maybe there was something more to this model and encouraging me to protect my work. Thank you to Michael, Bryan, Fernando, Owain, Michele, and Mariana for working with me to further refine TBO, the observation form, and the rubrics.

Thank you to the fantastic and friendly people at the two establishments where I wrote the book: Bluebeard Coffee and State Street Beer. I swear I only worked at State Street the last hour of the day. Thanks especially to Cody, Stephen, Dusty, and Alicia.

And thank you to Sarah Jubar, my acquisitions editor, who believed in the book and me. I am deeply grateful for your support.

I save my most special thanks for last, for my family. Thank you Acalia and Craig, the twins, for enduring and even thriving while I worked on the book. You guys amaze and impress me regularly. Most of all, thanks to my wife, Michele. I can never sufficiently express my thanks to the dedicated, talented, and loyal wife and educator you are, for your support and belief in me and *Trust-Based Observations*. When you loved the book is when I knew I had something.

Introduction

> Only principals equipped to handle a complex, rapidly changing environment can implement the reforms that lead to sustained improvement in student achievement.—Michael Fullan

"How come nobody observes me?" After a second consecutive year of not being observed by my principal, I was feeling more than a little frustrated. I knew I wanted someone, anyone, to observe me and more than the standard twice-a-year, pre-conference, observation, post-conference model. I craved more feedback on how to improve, and, truth be told, I wanted to demonstrate what I thought was good teaching. I wasn't alone. If you ask teachers about their experiences with the observation process, you are likely to hear comments like these:

- It's just a dog and pony show.
- They only saw me one time, then told me to get better at something that's a strength.
- I haven't been observed in one, two, three, four, or even five years.
- They didn't come in all year then brought me my end-of-year evaluation to sign. It was positive, but based on what?
- I get so nervous; they only see me at my worst. And my whole evaluation rests on it.
- They observed me but never gave me feedback. Arrggh.
- They e-mailed me my feedback. Talk about impersonal.

From these common refrains, one would think there is a better way of conducting observations, but what? Walkthroughs feel too short and impersonal. How can an observer get a real feel for a class and teacher in three to five minutes? I've done walkthroughs, and they feel too short to truly understand what's going on in class, plus they don't allow for seeing teaching transitions.

Traditional observations feel like nothing more than high-stakes evaluations, and principals don't get a real or deep impression of teachers when they observe them teaching classes only once or twice a year. Even if it's more than that, it doesn't feel like enough time to gain a sense of who each teacher is and of the teacher's strengths and growth areas. Most important, these observations don't feel like they're about improving teaching and learning; they feel like evaluations.

I wanted more; I wanted observations to be about becoming a better teacher. Experience had shown that teachers want to grow. There are exceptions, but most want to get better. I wanted to find a way to meaningfully tap into their desire for growth and support improved teaching and learning. Driven by this desire, I began my principal certification program.

As I started, though, I felt like something was wrong because I never heard anyone else share a desire for a better model. I heard complaints, but these were usually followed by "That's just the way it is." I felt my passion for observation was mine alone. I remember developing doubts about my beliefs; I recall feeling frustrated and a bit isolated. I was on the verge of accepting current models of observation as just the way it is.

Unlike most people I know working in education, as a kid I never had that one "make a difference" teacher who inspired me to teach. Instead, that "make a difference" mentor arrived when I needed it most. Warren Aller was the director of my principal certification program, and I could tell right away he wasn't a common thinker. His passion for his work was as clear as his kindness and caring heart. You could hear it and feel it in everything he said. Warren was honest, and every decision he made was based on the answer to what was best for kids.

Warren taught a number of my classes, and every one was a gift, but the class that made the biggest impact was "Supervision." During class, he drove home the point repeatedly that the key to improving teaching and learning was being in classes, observing teachers, having reflective conversations, and supporting teachers every day. Listening to him assert those beliefs for the first time was a Hallelujah moment. His words on observation resonated deeply; they felt right. I clearly remember a joyful, gut sense that this guy got it. My feeling of "Is it just me?" disappeared. I became a sponge, hanging on his every word.

Warren talked about being in classes every day, but I didn't know precisely what that meant. How much time were we supposed to be in class? I needed clarity. I vividly remember pushing him on the amount of time we were supposed to spend in classes. It took a while, I think, because like a naturally gifted teacher, Warren just did it without thinking about how much time he *actually* spent there. After a while, though, he said "an hour a day."

Although I was unaware of it at the time, that was the beginning of trust-based observations (TBO). Spend an hour a day observing teachers.

In the supervision class, we prepared by practicing observations over and over. We all brought in mini-lessons to teach to the class. We took turns, one of us teaching our lesson to the class and another observing, scripting the lesson, and taking notes. Following the lesson, we would simulate the reflective conversation, which always began by asking the same questions:

1. What were you doing to help students learn?
2. If you had it to do over again, what, if anything, would you change?

These questions still drive reflective talks today and became a key TBO element.

We received feedback from Warren on how we did, and we practiced more. We purposefully taught bad lessons and practiced responding to them. We practiced listening deeply. We practiced offering suggestions. We practiced dealing with defensive teachers. We left that course truly prepared to confidently conduct observations designed to help teachers grow.

However, would I be allowed to spend this much time observing in a world where an hour a day was definitely not the norm? As I began my principal career, I immediately realized I got lucky. I found myself working for Dave Christenbury, who was at a point in his career where the work that drove him was mentoring enthusiastic new principals. Passionate and full of ideas, every idea I brought to Dave was followed by "Is it good for kids?" and "What will it do to help kids learn?" Sound familiar? If my answers met his approval, I could go for it. I asked Dave if I could spend an hour a day doing twenty-minute teacher observations, and he said I could. He even decided to begin doing his observations this way. I was doing real observations.

As I began, I found myself feeling uncomfortable offering suggestions to teachers right away. Some of it was the new guy, wanting to be liked, and afraid of rocking the boat. Some of it was my fear of mistakenly offering a suggestion on a strength area and then losing teachers' trust because I told them to get better at something they were already good at doing. Some of it was this nagging feeling that it seemed so arrogant to watch somebody once or twice and then begin offering suggestions on such a tiny sample size. I had an uncomfortable feeling of "I don't know you yet; I'm not ready to offer suggestions until I really get a sense of you as a teacher."

So, instead of offering advice, after asking the questions, I began sharing what I noticed, meaning strengths in their teaching. All—or almost all—teachers have observable strengths, and it was usually easy to notice, be it relationships, pedagogy, or something else. Admittedly, there were a few moments where I had to search to find strengths, but I found them with everyone.

I soon discovered that I was onto something; teachers responded well to the "noticing" of strengths. They usually smiled and were genuinely happy, flattered, and sometimes embarrassed to have strengths shared with them. Strangely, before I even had a chance to offer suggestions, teachers began asking where they could get better. I don't mean a few teachers—I mean almost all of them.

Teachers asking about improving surprised me. It's not that I don't think teachers want to get better; I know they do. I just expected them to wait for me to offer suggestions. Somehow, because I had waited, they asked. Not aware at the time, focusing on strengths first and waiting to offer suggestions, led to the birth of another element of the TBO method. There were plenty of other early discoveries:

- There was a small percentage of teachers who were initially nervous during the reflective conversations. These teachers didn't want to talk much; they just wanted the conversation to be over. Their reasons varied. Some teachers are very self-critical, and some feel uncomfortable receiving feedback in general. Some teachers, based on past experiences, felt that because I was the principal, I must be out to get them. This worry is common among teachers based on experiences with principals trying to catch them doing things wrong. As time passed—and this point is important—virtually every teacher began to feel safe with the process and seemed to enjoy engaging in these reflective talks.
- Teachers were thankful to have someone observe them regularly. Many shared that in their entire careers, they had not been observed as much as they had in one year with us. This thankfulness drove home that teachers want to grow, be observed, and have conversations about improving.
- Some teachers were unaware of their strengths and were surprised to have them pointed out. I was shocked to have teachers do incredible things yet be unaware of what they were doing: "I do that? I don't know, it's just what I do" was a common response.
- Teachers were excited for collaborative growth opportunities. I had this sense, and many flat out said that this was the first time observations had been about getting better at teaching. Maybe it was because the experience was so new, maybe it was because they had a growth mindset but hadn't had the opportunity to work with their principal on improvement before, and maybe it was because I was "nice." Whatever the reason, teachers were genuinely enthusiastic about working on improving specific areas of their teaching.
- Teachers appreciated the trust-based style, and it influenced the way they felt about their principal. Teachers frequently stated that they felt sup-

ported by their principal for the first time in their careers. The reason was the positive, supportive, growth-oriented style of the observations. They liked being complimented and having their strengths noticed, they liked the reflective conversations, they liked feeling safe in the process, they liked that I was nice, and they liked supported opportunities for growth.

- I discovered who was really good at different elements of teaching. When administrators are in classes a lot, it becomes easy to identify who is an expert at specific areas of teaching. When we know who's really good at what, we can tap into these strengths to grow a whole faculty by having them lead professional development training. Without being in classes so much, there is no way to experientially know who is good at what. Huge benefits of noticing and tapping into teacher strengths are growing the capacity of an entire staff and the empowerment and development of teacher leaders.
- My experience shows that over 90 percent of teachers want to grow and are self-reflective. They're just looking for opportunities where they feel safe enough to take risks.

Before moving forward into the book, I feel compelled to share that I'm a practitioner more than a researcher. As such, I didn't research how to do observations *before* creating and practicing TBO. The model developed organically and evolved over time, mainly through intuition and trial and error. For the longest time, I didn't know I was developing an alternative model of observation. I just knew I wanted to be in classes a lot and help teachers get better.

Over time, as I experienced continued success with TBO, I felt compelled to formalize it. At first, I decided to speak at a conference and then to write an article. It was at this point that I decided it would be a good idea to start doing research. I did this research for two reasons:

1. In an effort to find empirical evidence of what I knew to be true, as suggested by Brown (2012)
2. To pull in and engage those who require (and justifiably so) empirical evidence in order to embrace change of the magnitude required to adopt TBO

My research disclaimer is that it was done largely ex post facto. Luckily, I found plenty of research supporting the elements of TBO that are different than traditional observations—the ones that are key to improving teaching and learning growth. For better or worse, I also found a plethora of evidence demonstrating why certain elements in many current and popular observation models work as obstacles to teaching and learning growth.

My hope is that this book will provide educational leaders with a manageable, step-by-step guide for fulfilling their top priority: measurably and meaningfully improving teaching and learning outcomes to unprecedented levels in every classroom in the world. So, after more than a decade of work, beginning with what I learned from Warren and developing, tweaking, failing, and adapting a multitude of times, I share TBO, the most powerful tool I know to improve teaching and learning.

CHAPTER OVERVIEW

As the book proceeds, in part 1, the obstacles to and solutions for using observation to support improved teaching and learning are shared. In chapter 1, the current problems with observations as they currently function are examined. The issues explored include teacher and principal feelings about observation: the dual design of current models of observation to both evaluate pedagogy and support teacher professional growth. Most important, and closely connected, is that teachers don't feel safe and trust the observation process or their principals enough. In chapter 2, the broad outline of solutions that form the core of TBO are shared. Particular emphasis is placed on the two most dramatic ideas surrounding improved observations and evaluations: the focus on observers intently focusing on building safe and trusting relationships with each of their teachers and eliminating the grading of pedagogy and replacing it with rating a teacher's mindset—growth or fixed.

Part 2 details how the process works from beginning to end. In chapter 3, the structure of the TBO system is explained. Included in the descriptions are the reasons behind the specifics of the system as well as troubleshooting tips. In chapter 4, the all-important elements that build TBO system success are discussed. Included are suggestions for creating, prioritizing, and managing the time required for the observations and reflective conversations, as well as the organization and personal accountability tools observers can use to support their TBO success.

Part 3 addresses all the details of TBO observations. Chapter 5 looks at the innovative observation form, its origins, development, and unique characteristics, including its manageability and use as a teacher-growth resource tool. Chapter 6 guides readers through the beginning "how-to" steps when starting an observation.

Chapter 7, the lengthiest chapter in the book, shares research supporting each of the areas of good teaching on the observation template. In addition, it guides readers on what to look for as an observer; it provides suggestions on how to use the observation form and what to write in each specific "Evidence of" category. Chapter 8 discusses the origins of each of the reflective conversation questions on the form and explains the rationale for using these questions to maximize teaching and learning. Finally, chapter 9 shows how the form doubles as a teacher professional development resource tool through the addition of Web links to the areas of pedagogy.

Part 4 details the most important part of the process: conducting successful follow-up conversations. It begins in chapter 10 by walking readers through all the steps involved, providing a clear overview of what the process looks like in practice. Chapter 11 provides a crucial guide on how to get the best out of your teachers through building trusting relationships with them. Actions that build trust are shared, as are those that inhibit trust. The role that vulnerability, mindset, and emotional intelligence play in building or eroding trust is also examined.

In chapter 12, the specifics of conducting a successful reflective conversation begins by guiding readers through asking the questions, becoming an effective active listener, reframing answers, and checking for clarity. In chapter 13, reflective conversation success continues by offering suggestions to observers on sharing "Evidence of," including how and what to share, with an emphasis on strengths and "noticing." Chapter 14 offers observers a guide on how and when to offer suggestions. As part of building suggestion success, the role of preparation, what and how much to suggest, using the right words, and explaining what continuing teacher support looks like and entails are also shared with readers. Finally, in chapter 15, observers are shown how to conduct special course connections accountability reflective conversations. These twice-yearly checks work to ensure alignment between unit plans, learning targets, actual teaching and learning, and summative assessments.

Part 5 addresses evaluation and professional development. In chapter 16, the teacher self-assessment rubric, its criterion levels, and how to have teachers use the tool are explained. In addition, action research big goals are explained, as is teacher guidance for creating the goals. Chapter 17 details the evaluation process for TBO; the rubric is shared and explained as observers are guided on evaluating teachers in the areas of collegiality and communication, professionalism, preparation and planning, and mindset.

Action improvement plans and difficult conversations are discussed in chapter 18. This chapter details the values of teachers besides teaching, supporting growth so that plans are no longer necessary, the role of preparation in creating the plans, and success tips for talking with teachers about the plans. It also discusses difficult conversations, overcoming fight-or-flight responses, and empathy for teachers. Chapter 19 connects professional development directly to TBO pedagogy. Ways to empower teacher leaders while growing faculty capabilities through the "question of the year" and TBO pedagogy linked to professional development communities are shared.

Finally, part 6 provides guidance on successfully implementing and sustaining success with TBO.

Part 1

Observation Problems and Solutions

Chapter One

So What's the Problem?

What is needed is a radical re-think, a change of mindset about what observations are for and what they can do to support classroom practice and students' learning.—Matt O'Leary

So what's the problem? The problem is that observations aren't working. Most teachers don't really like being observed, most principals don't really enjoy doing observations, and, most important, research evidence shows that observations are not improving teaching or student learning outcomes. The reality is that observations often end up doing the opposite of what they're supposed to do. Instead of helping teachers grow and improve their practice, the process of evaluating pedagogy, combined with the absence of an atmosphere of support, causes teachers to play it safe. They fear getting something wrong and being evaluated negatively because of a mistake. They fear experiencing negative job repercussions as a result of poor ratings, so they don't take chances, and teachers don't get better without taking risks.

Teachers don't like being observed. Based on personal experience and stories that teachers have relayed to me, there are two major causes of teacher frustration with the observation process. The first is the infrequent nature of observations combined with evaluatively graded post-observation conferences. Partially because of the rarity of observations, follow-up conversations are a painful exercise in vulnerability where teachers listen to principals highlight what was wrong and offer an unmanageable number of suggestions for improvement. Although this is not everyone's experience, it feels like that to many.

The second frustration for teachers is their feeling of not being supported. When speaking with teachers anecdotally, on average they say that between one-third and two-thirds of the principals they have worked for have not been supportive during observations. Current models of observation play a significant role in causing these negative perceptions, but there are other principal actions responsible too, including the following:

- Neglecting to do the minimum standard of one or two observations per year
- E-mailing or not giving feedback   No email
- Possessing a generally negative disposition
- Alienating teachers by conveying a message that principals know how to do it better
- Forgetting how difficult being a teacher is and showing no empathy for their challenges
- Making permanent snap judgments about teachers based on a single observation
- Not using emotional intelligence to interact with their teachers in constructive ways
- Forcing "their way" to teach as the only way to be effective

Principals don't enjoy the process of doing observations either. Many feel that it's a necessary evil, a duty to be done, a box to be checked off, and so they are strategically compliant. Many feel that cumbersome state requirements and strict observation frameworks interfere with the real work of helping teachers improve. Most want to help teachers improve; it's just that the evaluative process as it currently functions makes it difficult to do so. In most models, visits are infrequent yet time consuming. They rate teachers on an inordinately large number of areas, share findings, and give advice. The infrequency of visits makes meaningful dialogue about progress and next steps difficult. How can you observe someone months later and then provide constructive feedback on progress?

Finally, the evidence on the effectiveness of observations is not good. Despite intense efforts and huge sums of money spent, the work done in previous decades to strengthen the evaluation process has not resulted in meaningful measured improvement in teaching and student learning. Most compellingly, the most thorough, long-lasting effort to use evaluation to improve learning and graduation rates has failed to achieve its goals.

This Gates Foundation–funded initiative to improve teacher effectiveness was aimed at dramatically increasing students' access to effective teaching and, as a result, improving student outcomes. The Rand Corporation evaluated the effectiveness of the initiative, and after seven years of work using the evaluation process to improve student achievement, the results were largely unsuccessful. Despite spending more than $200 million implementing improved measures of teacher effectiveness, there was no significant and sustained teacher or student performance improvement (Stecher et al. 2018). No wonder teachers and principals don't like observations—all this effort and nothing to show for it.

WHAT CAN BE DONE

With not many people really liking the process and data making it clear that current methods aren't improving teaching and learning, an examination of teacher observation and evaluation is in order. Discoveries can be made about what did and didn't work in the past, what is and isn't working now, and the reasons why. This information can be used to develop a model that does what it's supposed to do, namely, to continually improve teaching as well as student learning outcomes. Personal experience has shown that observations can be a principal's most effective tool in supporting growth albeit only with the radical rethink and change of mindset that O'Leary writes about at the beginning of the chapter.

One thing that's known is that principals must be instructional leaders if they are to be the effective leaders needed for sustained innovation—the crucial variable affecting instructional quality and student achievement. At the heart, are principals focused on the development of teachers (Fullan 2002). In essence, a principal's chief responsibility is doing everything possible to support and optimize the growth of teaching and learning, just like a teacher's job is to do everything possible to maximize student learning and development.

Now, add to the principal's role as instructional leader the insight that leading authorities provide on effective observations practice: teacher evaluation systems need to be designed and implemented with teacher learning and development at their core (Marzano and Toth 2013). Charlotte Danielson said, "Doing it well means respecting what we know about teacher learning, which has to do with self-assessment, reflections on practice, and professional conversation. And when you do those things, you have enormous growth" (Hess 2011).

So principal roles and responsibilities, as well as goals and actions to take, are known. What's getting in the way of success? Two partially connected problems are interfering with observation effectiveness. The first is the widespread desire for observations to serve the dual purposes of supporting the professional growth of teachers while also evaluatively grading them. The problem with the duality is that rating teachers inhibits their growth; as soon as an evaluative or a developmental rating of pedagogy enters the picture, teachers become cautious and fearful and stop taking risks.

Research makes it clear that there has been a nullifying impact on innovation with graded observations that resulted in a decline in the creativity in teachers' practice, as they feared taking risks: the summative grade became

an obstacle rather than an opportunity for teachers to further their professional learning (O'Leary 2017). So, despite warnings for schools to ensure that
the accountability system does not undermine professional growth (Good and
Brophy 2003), that's exactly what's happening.

The second problem preventing observations from improving teaching
and learning gets to the core of trust-based observations: teachers don't feel
safe or supported. There are a number of reasons that they don't feel safe or
supported. One reason is the evaluative ratings. An even bigger reason is that
leader actions aren't focused enough on creating safe and trusting relationships with their teachers. Teachers must trust you and feel safe in order to
willingly take risks and try new things. The truth is that legitimacy begins
with trust: nothing will move until trust is firm (Greenleaf 2002). Without
feelings of trust and safety, especially when supervisors have power over
decisions regarding retention, innovation, risk taking, and meaningful growth
are unlikely to occur.

Pointing out the important role that trust plays in success is not new. Calls
for "trust" to build more successful schools, businesses, and relationships
have been steady in previous decades. Anthony Bryk, coauthor of *Trust in
Schools* and president of the Carnegie Foundation for the Advancement of
Teaching, wrote, "Relational trust is a vital but neglected factor in school
success . . . absent such relational trust building, improvements in the quality
of schooling remain very unlikely" (Bryk and Schneider 2002). Parker Palmer (2017), educator, activist, and author of *The Courage to Teach*, wrote,
"Who does not know that you can throw the best methods, the latest equip-
ment, and a lot of money at people who do not trust each other and still get
miserable results? Who does not know that people who trust each other and
work well together can do exceptional work with less than adequate resources?" Matt O'Leary (2017), lecturer, researcher, and editor and author of
Reclaiming Lesson Observation, wrote, "For any initiative set to improve
quality in teaching and learning to have impact there must, at the heart, be
trust." Jon Gordon (2017), leadership expert and author of *The Power of
Positive Leadership*, wrote, "Leading is . . . about investing in relationships,
bringing out the best in others, coaching, encouraging, serving, caring, and
being someone that your team can trust. People you lead ask, 'Can I trust
you?' To be someone people want to follow, you have to be someone they
can trust."

The good news is that, as school leaders, you have the power to overcome
the obstacles in the observation process that inhibit the growth of teaching
and improved student learning outcomes. You can take a new path and the
steps necessary to build trusting relationships with your teachers such that
they embrace risk taking in their practice. The hope in sharing trust-based
observations is that you choose to implement this new schema-changing

model, a model of observation that fosters improved teaching and improved student performance.

Chapter Two

The Solution

Trust-Based Observations

The goal of trust-based observations (TBO) is to eliminate the problem with observations, that they do *not* improve teaching and learning. Developing successful answers to this problem does involve a radical rethinking—a schema change—about (1) what observations are designed to do and (2) the steps used to reach improvement. Vital to these shifts in thinking and action must be a concrete core belief that improvement happens when people persist in taking risks and trying practices that are new to them; in other words, they innovate. For principals, the aim then is to create the conditions that encourage teachers to construe their teaching in terms of a series of related experimental designs (risk taking) (Hattie 2008). For teachers to enthusiastically embrace taking these chances, ingredients that cultivate the confidence to take risks must be added and obstacles that interfere with risk taking eliminated.

To create these conditions, successful observation approaches previously developed or suggested but somehow forgotten will be reinvigorated and added, and new approaches and ideas consciously designed to provide maximum support for teacher risk taking and growth will be added. In addition, the inclusion of a major modification to the "evaluation" portion of observations is also made so that it encourages instead of inhibits innovation and risk taking. In combining all of these elements, the use of the observation process to consistently and continually improve teaching and student learning becomes a reality. This chapter explores these conditions and solutions.

BUILD SAFE, TRUSTING RELATIONSHIPS

Chief among the steps that create conditions for risk taking is developing trust with teachers such that they feel comfortable engaging in reflective conversations with you in order to grow their practice. The goal is for teachers to feel safe enough that they willingly take chances trying new things and safe enough that they know it will be okay even if their efforts don't turn out the way they desire. You want to develop an atmosphere where teachers can try and fail and know that they will still be supported, even embraced, for taking risks.

When teachers trust their principal and feel safe, they are more willing to absorb the inevitable ups and downs that accompany developing new or improved practice. When observers honor the scary endeavor that is risk taking, it lessens teachers' fears and anxieties associated with taking chances. Creating a safe atmosphere helps them take action; because they are supported, they feel that the potential reward outweighs their fear.

Michael Fullan (2002), researcher, education reformer, leadership expert, and author of *The Change Leader*, backs these beliefs, writing that "ensuring deeper learning requires mobilizing the energy and capacities of teachers. To mobilize teachers, we must improve teachers' working conditions and morale. One of the essential components of improving working conditions and morale is the ability to improve relationships. In fact, the single factor common to successful change is that relationships improve. If relationships improve, schools get better. If relationships remain the same or get worse, ground is lost. Thus, leaders build relationships."

Throughout the history of teacher observations, the importance of relationships as they relate to success as well as calls for actions to build relationships have been regular:

- In the 1950s, school administrator and writer Ethel Thompson (1952), without knowing it, addressed the importance of using emotional intelligence to build relationships, writing that the ability to work with human material, ingenuity, a sense of humor, and interest in people is mandatory in this work.
- In the 1960s, Robert Goldhammer, one of the developers of the clinical model of teacher supervision and coauthor of *Clinical Supervision*, touched on the importance of an increased frequency in the number of observations as a key element in building relationships when he wrote about "a continuous cycle of observations with a focus on building a trusting rapport between teacher and supervisor" (Goldhammer et al. 1993).

- At the turn of the twenty-first century, Bryk and Schneider (2002) highlighted the centrality of relational trust in school improvement, specifically to measured improvements in academic productivity.
- More recently, John Hattie (2008), researcher and author of *Visible Learning*, addressed "safe," writing that "teachers themselves need to be in a safe environment to learn about the success or otherwise of their teaching from others." He adds to the importance of trust, writing that "it maximizes the occurrence of error and thus allows feedback to be powerful in use and effectiveness."
- Finally, O'Leary (2014) suggests "honoring the importance of building a trusting relationship between observer and observee."

These calls to build relationships are not new, but either the focus on relationship is not a regular part of observation practice or its importance is not highlighted enough. Over the course of this book, readers will see TBO examine and share how to build these elements into their observation practice. Building these relationships with teachers takes awareness, time, organization, and purposeful effort and are briefly touched on here.

First, it's crucial that observers have an understanding of and empathy for the complete vulnerability of the observation process for teachers. There is no other job where the boss comes into the employee's office, as it were, sits down, and watches her work while taking notes on what he sees. The boss then leaves, and the employee has to wait and worry until the boss is ready to meet to tell her what he thinks of the work he witnessed. That's the best-case scenario. For many people, the feedback is purely one way via an e-mail they receive. As a supervisor, using one's empathy to understand this vulnerable process and to guide words and tone used in interactions with teachers is an important start in helping to build relationships.

Next is an understanding that the best time to build relationships and put empathy to use is during face-to-face follow-up conversations with teachers, meaning that an increased focus must be placed on these reflective talks. There is much potential in these conversations for the principal, as instructional leader, to foster supported professional growth when purposeful time and effort are spent building trust. During these conversations, elements that principals use to build relationship include the following:

- Asking specifically designed, purposefully reflective questions to teachers
- Listening intently
- Focusing on teacher strengths
- Developing and using emotional intelligence
- Honoring teaching intangibles
- Differentiating the conversations to each teacher's personality, strengths, and growth areas

- Channeling their best and most empathetic "nice"

Time will be devoted over the course of this book to expand on these specific "how-to's." Learning these relationship-building tools and skills is invaluable because well-established relationships are the resource that keeps on giving (Fullan 2002).

Finally, these tools and skills successfully build relationships that influence growth only when significant time is spent with teachers. Continuing feedback works when it's frequent enough that the previous visit is still relatively fresh in both people's minds. So, the observations have to cycle through quickly yet still be manageable. TBO provides a specific and manageable schedule of twelve twenty-minute observations per week with subsequent reflective conversations the next day. Tied to the success of maintaining these visits are organization and time management steps, which will be illuminated in future chapters.

Building trusting relationships, however, is not the only answer. Building relationships helps teachers feel a greater sense of safety, something that's vital on the path to embracing risk taking. More can be done, though. To be most effective, the observation process has to also minimize the fear that teachers feel. Although trusting relationships reduce fear, they don't eliminate it. Fear is not eliminated because a teacher's pedagogy is evaluated (or rated). If, however, teachers don't have to worry about their pedagogy being graded, then fear can more fully dissipate.

TWEAK EVALUATION

Realistically, it's hard to imagine that there will ever be a time when evaluation is not connected to the observation process. Retention decisions will always have to be made for teaching personnel, as in any job, and since on-the-job performance is a large determinant of workplace success, how can observation of teachers at work not be part of those decisions? There is a way, however, to successfully include evaluation as part of the observation process without its contributing to the "play it safe," fear-based mindset that inhibits the risk taking necessary for the growth of teaching and learning. Eliminate the grading/rating of pedagogy from evaluation and replace it with something else.

Why eliminate the rating of pedagogy? The act of rating teacher pedagogical skills causes fear, which induces a cautious mindset, which in turn inhibits a teacher's willingness to take risks. As long as pedagogy is rated, risk taking will be suppressed and the growth of teaching minimal. As O'Leary's (2017) research found, "The grade became an obstacle rather than an opportunity for teachers to further their professional learning. Grades did nothing to progress individual teacher development or noticeably improve the organisation."

In response, some will say that their rubrics are a measurement scale; they provide a leveled continuum of skill development that provides a path forward for teachers' next steps. Some will say that the numbers or leveled rating labels are insignificant; they're just words or numbers. Some will say that they are developmental ratings, not evaluative grades. No matter how their use of pedagogical rubrics is described, they feel like critical measurements to teachers, and that matters because the result is reduced risk taking.

There is no doubt that the details described in the different developmental levels of rubrics do provide for the possibility of helping to develop skills. The problem is that when these rating evaluations come from outside oneself, in largely infrequent doses, the ability to help promote growth diminishes rapidly because the ratings are perceived critically. Addressing potential naysayers, of course, there are a small percentage of teachers who don't mind the "critical" evaluative approach, especially when delivered gently and even more so when a trusting relationship is built. For most teachers, though, one of two things happen:

1. They shut down or play it safe and don't take risks because of the vulnerability involved and the fear that develops from "evaluation."
2. They will be compliant in their actions but not willingly or passionately, so the odds of sustained growth diminish. Effectiveness is limited and usually not sustained because it wasn't born of a trusting relationship or one's own choices for growth.

Perception is reality, and the perception is that they are being judged.

The good news is that the evaluation of pedagogy in individual and end-of-year evaluations can be eliminated, yet effective and accurate indicators of performance necessary to guide retention decisions can still be made. So, what is evaluated then? Nobody has complained that it's unfair to evaluate planning and preparation, professionalism, or collegiality and collaboration; they are necessary elements that play into the success of almost any job.

What else, though? What can help ensure good teaching and teaching improvement if pedagogy isn't evaluated? The answer lies within the TBO reflective conversations. In those visits, once teachers feel safe, observers learn crucial information that speaks to a teacher's potential for improvement. Observers are able to assess and measure a teacher's willingness to take the steps necessary for improvement, information that proves a more accurate tool for evaluating and promoting growth than the evaluation of pedagogy.

So, the big evaluative change is eliminating the measurement of pedagogy and replacing it with the measurement of a teacher's mindset. In evaluating mindset, it's possible to determine a teacher's thoughts and beliefs on self-improvement, a very telling measure. With a fixed mindset, the accompanying resistance inhibits change, risk taking, innovation, and thus improvement. With a growth mindset, improvement is not only possible but also probable because trial and error is embraced. By substituting mindset for pedagogy, insight is gained into this desire to improve, including a teacher's willingness to do whatever is necessary for increased student success.

This insight is gained without the emotional charge that comes with evaluating teachers' pedagogical skills. Just the act of evaluating mindset encourages risk taking. Add in safe, trusting relationships, and the result is usually an embrace of risk taking. Ultimately, if the result of this change is teachers taking more risks to improve their practice, then isn't it worth it?

A radical change? Yes, but evidence says that rating pedagogy inhibits improvement; evidence says that observations are not improving teaching and learning. So why not work to eliminate a major obstacle to growth?

Although the hope is that every district, school, and principal will adopt the replacement of evaluating pedagogy with evaluating mindset, the reality is that hope won't manifest itself everywhere immediately. So, adopt it with your district. If that's not possible, pilot it with your district. If that's not possible, pilot it with your school. If that's not possible, pilot it with some teachers in your school. If that's not possible, at a minimum, limit the rating of pedagogy to only the end-of-year evaluation. If that's not possible, adopt all the other elements of TBO and be the most supportive and trusting principal your teachers have ever worked with in their careers. Build trust and encourage their risk taking; do everything possible to make teachers feel safe.

To share a final thought on eliminating the evaluative rating of pedagogy: doing so doesn't mean getting rid of the rubrics, just using them differently. The rubrics have value for teachers as a self-assessment tool, to guide next steps in development, and in discussions with observers about growth. Used for these purposes, pedagogical rubrics don't inhibit teacher risk taking; rather, they foster reflection and individual professional development growth decisions. Observers just don't use them to measure individual pedagogical development anymore.

ADDITIONAL SOLUTIONS

Finally, beyond building safe and trusting relationships with each teacher and rating mindset instead of pedagogy, there are many other purposeful design elements necessary to making TBO a comprehensive solution that improves teaching and student learning. Over the course of this book, these pieces of the puzzle will be expanded on in detail. As a brief preview, though, some of these elements are:

- Observations are unannounced, providing a more authentic look at teaching.
- Pre-observation conferences are eliminated, freeing up extra time to do the observations.
- All teachers are observed equally each year because it sends a message about lifelong learning and because observers learn from the strongest teachers, improving the school and empowering those teachers.
- A manageable observation form still addresses important areas of teaching success.
- An observation form functions as a learning resource tool for teachers and observers alike by listing Web-linked "Toolbox Possibilities." Listing these possibilities serves two purposes: it guides observers in using precise language to describe a strategy, and the Web links allow teachers to quickly access resources that help them build their skills.
- Observations include student interviews to check for alignment between intended learning targets and actual student learning.
- A direct connection is made between observation areas of pedagogy and professional development.
- Periodic reflective conversation accountability checks ensure alignment between course curriculum, learning targets, and summative assessments.
- Guidance is provided to support TBO implementation and maintenance success.

Together, all of these solutions, expanded on in the rest of this book, provide the comprehensive package of solutions that is TBO.

Part 2

The TBO System and Making It Work

Chapter Three

The System Basics

*Continuous, Frequent, Unannounced,
and Short Observations*

To effectively implement TBO, it's important to have a clear understanding of the system and the reasoning behind it. To that end, one of the keys to the success of TBO is its method of continuous, frequent, unannounced, and short visits. Building safe and trusting relationships with teachers—a key factor in developing innovative, risk-taking teacher mindsets—takes time, so a continuous cycle of frequent observations plays a crucial role in cultivating these relationships.

When principals observe classes repeatedly, they really get to know their teachers and the teachers' personalities, strengths, and areas for growth. By engaging in regular reflective conversations, they demonstrate a genuine interest in their teachers and their practice, which builds safe and trusting relationships, which then fosters risk taking and growth. None of this is possible with infrequent visits.

The big question is, what does "frequent" mean? Lately, most observation models speak of "frequent" or "more" but neglect to provide particulars, leaving principals frustrated. In TBO, the answer is clear: principals observe all teachers equally, even the stars and part-timers, operating on a continuous cycle of twelve unannounced, twenty-minute observations per week, followed by equally short reflective conversations the next day. Besides providing frequency clarity, the system provides principals with time, a primary tool for establishing relationships and effectively supporting growth.

TBO discovered (through trial and error) that twenty-four purposeful observation-related teacher interactions per week is the perfect feasible amount of visits for principals to maintain as part of their practice. In a normal five-day workweek the cycle is as follows:

Monday: three observations
Tuesday–Thursday: three observations and three reflective conversations
Friday: three reflective conversations

As TBO worked to design the maximum number of visits that principals could sustain, it became apparent that the gap between Friday observations and Monday reflective conversations was too long to make the reflections productive. Even with detailed notes, it was difficult for principals to recall the observation clearly. For teachers, with all the different classes they teach, remembering details from one class three days prior was next to impossible. As a result, Friday observations were eliminated. The best part of this change was the unanticipated benefit. Fewer visits on Monday and Friday made the schedule more manageable. These lighter days provided principals with more time to schedule administrative work and meetings on Mondays and Fridays, making the busier Tuesdays, Wednesdays, and Thursdays more tenable.

TBO's system of continuously visiting a set number of teachers each week as opposed to observing teachers once, twice, or more per year represents a significant schema shift. Calendaring twenty-four visits per week actually proves easier to manage as well. Like Kevin Kruse (2016), professor and best-selling author, writes in *15 Surprising Things Productive People Do Differently*, "They put things on their calendars and then work and live from that calendar. It sounds like a pain, but this will set you up in the 95th percentile." That's what TBO in essence does: calendar twenty-four visits per week. The routine of this schedule helps observers immensely in maintaining the cycle of visits.

The time commitment for visits has proven sustainable. The observations are twenty minutes, plus time to get to and from class. The reflective conversations take ten to twenty minutes. In addition to the roughly ten minutes it takes to organize the daily schedule, the observation process takes a little over an hour on Mondays and Fridays and a little over two hours on Tuesdays through Thursdays. Knowing that this time spent with teachers leads to genuine improvement in teaching and learning, it is the most productive eight to ten hours per week a principal can spend.

Although the cycle is manageable, one of the biggest challenges for observers—yet keys to success—is and always will be continuing to get the visits done on a daily basis. Time is almost always an issue for principals, but there is more to maintaining the cycle than just creating time.

Sustaining the visits comes down to a combination of establishing a routine, making it a habit, creating a sense of urgency to get the visits done *every* day, and holding and being held to account for doing the visits. It's like working out. There are days when it's easy to get the visits done because motivation is there. There are days when the desire to do the visits just isn't there. On these days, an obligation to improved teaching and learning, sheer will, and knowing that observers are being held to account for completing the visits have to be used to get them done.

Maintaining the cycle of visits is never conquered. Daily diligence is required, along with the ability to forgive oneself on days when all the visits aren't completed. Observers will find themselves more motivated to continue their cycle of visits as relationships with teachers develop, as they really get to know their teachers, and, most important, as they start to see improvements in teaching. Every day, though, a conscious choice must be made to do the visits. The rewards will be there when principals maintain the cycle.

Regarding the system, there are four important "why" questions to answer.

Why Unannounced?

Unannounced observations provide more accurate and authentic pictures of teaching and learning than announced observations. Even in the best circumstances, with the most dedicated teacher, it is human nature to put extra effort into preparation when they know they are going to be observed. The result is that the observer is not seeing an authentic representation of normal day-to-day teaching. It does no good to see an inaccurate picture of what's going on in class. Observations are about the growth of teaching and learning; seeing an inauthentic picture of teaching doesn't foster the growth of teaching and has the potential to inhibit student learning. Observers have to see the real thing in order to help.

Unannounced visits provide accountability. It's surprising how many teachers say they like knowing that observations are unannounced. These teachers often report that it helps them ensure that they stay on top of their teaching game knowing that a visit is coming but not knowing when. They feel they perform better knowing that they are being held to account via a form of intermittent reinforcement. Part of observation is making sure that what's being taught is of a certain quality and aligns with the curriculum. Unannounced visits help provide this accountability.

Why a Continuous Cycle?

For starters, the manner in which observations are conducted under the current system makes them laughably insufficient—current classroom observations are far too infrequent to be informative (Winters 2012). Besides increasing the number of visits, people function better in routines. The routine of a continuous cycle is easier to maintain than the periodic observations of traditional models. In these models, because of the infrequency of visits and no set schedule, determining when to do them is challenging and often ends up feeling more like fitting them in.

Ask teachers, and they will give at least one example of a school year when it felt like the principal was just getting in the observation before the end of the school year, not purposefully seeing them. When principals adhere to a continuous cycle, however, they are continuing a pattern of working their way through another round of visits. There is less to think about in a continuous cycle: just the visits for today.

Principals really get to know their teachers when they see them with the frequency that the TBO continuous cycle provides. When observers are continually in classes and having reflective conversations, they genuinely know their teachers. They know their strengths and their growth areas. They learn who has superior skills in a particular pedagogical area. They use this information, tapping into teacher strengths for the purposes of professional development. There is no way observers could discover these experts who support schoolwide growth without the frequency that a continuous cycle provides.

Principals can better support teacher growth as they take risks on new practice. When teachers try new strategies, they want—and it is important for them to receive—coaching feedback on the progress of their new initiative so that tweaks or adjustments can be made if necessary. Meaningful timely feedback given in a continuous cycle of visits is simply not possible when observing teachers infrequently and irregularly. As Richard Stiggins and Daniel Duke (1988), authors of *The Case for Commitment to Teacher Growth*, noted, "A continuous cycle of feedback . . . is needed to promote teacher development."

Principals can accurately address parental concerns from a place of knowledge. When principals follow a continuous cycle of visits, they are in classes frequently enough that when a parent brings up a concern, principals can speak with great authority about their teachers and their classes. Sometimes these parental concerns are legitimate, and sometimes they are not. Either way, it is so much more satisfying and reassuring as a principal to be able to address these concerns with the knowledge that one possesses from being in classes regularly. Knowing teachers this well is simply not possible without a continuous cycle of visits.

Teachers enjoy being observed more frequently. Most teachers report, maybe surprisingly, that they actually like knowing that their administrator is coming into their class a lot. Over time, as they feel comfortable and safe, they look forward to the opportunity for feedback and to show off what they are doing well. A continuous cycle of visits provides these opportunities, ones that traditional models don't offer teachers.

"Continuous" models lifelong learning. Observers keep plugging away, doing visits with teachers. Both persevere to improve student outcomes, creating a lifelong learning loop that is an excellent model for students, one that is just not possible with infrequent observations.

Why Twenty Minutes?

Time spent in class has to be long enough that a meaningful picture of teaching and learning is observable. Obtaining that in less than twenty minutes while also interviewing students on their learning, one of the unique accountability pieces of TBO, is not manageable. Twenty minutes has proven enough time to gain a picture of the class while also interviewing students.

The time must also be short enough that the frequency of visits necessary to influence growth is still manageable for observers. Twenty minutes, within the continuous cycle of twenty-four visits per week, has shown to be an ideal time for maintaining frequency and meaning.

Why Observe All Teachers Equally?

By observing all teachers equally—which doesn't mean that teachers on improvement plans aren't observed more often—principals send a valuable message about the importance of "lifelong learning" as it relates to observation; it's for everyone. By observing all teachers equally every year, observers maintain accountability and knowledge of teaching and learning in every class and have the opportunity to continually help support the growth of all teachers, even expert and part-time teachers.

Many models provide observation plans that include teachers not being observed in particular years. Some people think expert teachers don't require observation, but in observing all teachers, principals create better schools. Besides discovering teaching mastery, reflective conversations with teachers who otherwise might not be observed often veer into philosophical discussions where ideas are shared that lead to new initiatives that grow the whole school.

When everyone isn't observed or observed equally, sometimes jealousies develop that interfere with collegiality among a faculty. By observing everyone equally, an environment more conducive to cooperation and collegiality is developed and maintained.

TROUBLESHOOTING

As principals implement TBO, there are common questions that observers have regarding the system's cycle of visits. Knowing the answers helps observers be more successful.

How do I manage the observations during a nontraditional workweek? When there is a Monday or Friday holiday, follow the same process but shorten it by one day. On a midweek day off, the process still works fine with one extra day in between observation and reflective conversation, so modify the schedule accordingly. On half days, the recommendation is to use these days to do the reflective conversations from the day before and then either do a manageable number of observations or skip observations that day and catch up on other duties.

What do I do if I don't get all the visits in on a particular day? There are two main reasons visits don't happen: some type of school emergency arises that requires all of a principal's time, or a principal just didn't get them done. Such is the unpredictable life of a principal that there will be days where emergencies arise that literally prevent getting all the visits done. When crazy days happen, don't try to make up the observations the next day. Over time, trying to make up a missed observation or two proves unmanageable; a hole develops that is difficult to dig out of, frustration increases, and the hole gets deeper, sometimes leading to not doing visits at all. Instead of trying to make up the missed visit, chalk it up to a nutty day and start fresh tomorrow.

On occasion, visits don't take place because principals couldn't will themselves to do some of their visits that day. The author has never had a year when this did not happen. The best advice is for observers to forgive themselves and start fresh the next day. Get back on that horse.

A key step in getting all the visits in is to do the first observation or reflective conversation in the first period. The pattern has begun, and the rest of the day becomes easier, even when crazy things happen later in the day. All principals know that crazy happens frequently, so getting as many visits as possible done early helps combat the unpredictability of a principal's day.

What do I do if I keep missing a teacher for the reflective conversation? First, the best way to avoid missing a reflective conversation is to prioritize them when creating the daily schedule. Reflective conversations can occur only before or after school or on a teacher's one or two prep periods. Because the window for these conversations is smaller than for observations, schedule them first and as early in the day as possible. If there is a teacher to observe and a reflective conversation to be had the same period, visit the reflective conversation teacher first.

It's also true that despite best efforts, there will be times when an observer goes into a teacher's room and the teacher isn't there. Although there is no surefire answer that works all the time, the best advice after missing the teacher all day is to e-mail them to schedule a meeting either before school, during a prep, or after school the next day. Look at your schedule, provide options, and let them make the choice.

When more than two days have passed since the observations (this does occur on rare occasions), principals have to make a decision about what to do. TBO's best recommendation is to let the teacher know that multiple efforts were made to meet with them and then provide the teacher with the option of still meeting or waiting until the next round of observations. Teachers appreciate that their principal is giving them the choice, providing at a minimum another opportunity to build relationship.

Is it okay to take a day off from doing observations? No, and yes. Taking a day off can easily turn into taking two days off, interfering with the habit of getting in the visits. Therefore, it's dangerous to take a day off. At the same time, there are days when the amount of time necessary for a big project with an impending due date is so great that all time must be spent on those efforts. In those instances, when the time commitment is real and necessary, it is okay to take a day off. Just start observing again the next day.

What if I'm just not getting the visits done? The frequency of visits is new for most principals, and therefore adapting to the cycle can be challenging. Worries about having reflective conversations—even positive, strengths-based ones—can interfere with doing visits. These worries are compounded when thinking about challenging teachers. Remember that teachers are often worried about the new model as well. Getting into classes and having these reflective conversations is part of the invaluable process of building relationships. Be driven by the desire to have all the principal's actions be about doing what's best for kids.

Finally, use accountability. If there are assistant principals, hold each other to account by having daily checks on visits done. Use principal supervisors; have them check regularly and ask for evidence. Use whatever works.

Chapter Four

Building System Success

Creating Time and Getting Organized

One of the great joys for many principals is the job's unpredictability, where the only certainty from day to day is that something unexpected is likely to happen. Boredom from monotony is not likely to be a principal's complaint. The flip side, however, is that because of these unexpected events that pop up on a near-daily basis, successfully completing all of the duties associated with the job is difficult and may not even be possible. This is why it is so common to hear principals express concerns about not having enough time to do observations. It's common for principals to express frustrations that

- evaluations are time intensive and difficult to implement given principals' other work,
- they were required to evaluate too many teachers each year, and
- the paperwork demands with their district evaluation process are very extensive.

Some administrators reported that they found it necessary to shortcut parts of the process just to complete even the most basic elements (Kersten and Israel 2005).

It's important to remember that these complaints are for *traditional observations* that require pre-conferences, observing an entire period, lengthy evaluative write-ups, and formal evaluative post-conferences requiring ratings discussions and improvement suggestions for an incredibly large number of teaching indicators. In traditional models, such suggestions mean that the next time observers see them, it might be months later or even the next year, and most likely these have been forgotten by both parties by the next visit. No wonder principals are frustrated.

Who, be it teacher or principal, would want to spend time engaging in this futile activity? It's no wonder that principals complain about the time required. The work is resulting not in improvement but merely in checking off boxes and completing a chore. Teachers provide strategically compliant answers, and everyone knows what is going on—a duty fulfilled by parties in a play designed to fool the audience into thinking that the result is improved teaching and learning.

CREATING AND PRIORITIZING TIME

If there were another way to do observations that felt fun, meaningful, impactful, and less formal, then what would change? Because time spent in observations felt worthwhile, principals would prioritize them. TBO provides this change, but managing the time necessary for the observations is not a given simply because the new process improves teaching and learning outcomes. Navigating the time to successfully maintain the schedule of classroom visits takes organization and prioritization, which means developing ways to lighten the load.

Managing all of a principal's responsibilities successfully will always be a challenge. There is no way to do "everything." The job is a continual to-do list that will never be finished. Knowing and accepting this reality helps lessen anxiety and helps the principal plug away a day at a time. What else helps? Prioritizing; there are deadlines, and, at times, these must be met. Besides deadlines, what is most important? That which is most likely to improve student learning outcomes, which means putting in the observation time. To successfully manage time for the visits, there are strategies and tips that can be used to create and maintain the necessary time. These are discussed in the following sections.

Routine

First, the continuous cycle of visits helps one manage time more effectively. Think about summers as a teacher. Often the lack of routine feels great at first but then wears old within weeks. Humans crave and function better in routines. Now compare TBO's cycle of continuous visits to more traditional models. Because the visits are a weekly routine, it's easier to do them; the regularity becomes a habit. When required to get in one or two visits per year (sometimes more), the infrequent nature of traditional observations actually makes it more difficult to do them because there is no schedule, no routine.

As an added bonus, the visit routine makes you more effective in your dealings with teachers because habitualness creates mood, which creates the "nurture" aspect of your personality (Wiest 2018). Think about the ber... Routine creates a nurturing mood, which builds relationships, which creates safety, which creates the conditions for risk taking.

Squeeze Them In

There are lots of twenty-minute time windows during the course of the day; use these to do a visit. Kim Marshall (2013), editor of *The Marshall Memo* and author of *Rethinking Teacher Supervision and Evaluation*, wrote, "It was most efficient to fit in my visits between other errands and expeditions around the school. Sometimes I was successful in blocking out a whole period for classroom visits, but that amount of time rarely went by without something else coming up. Mostly I squeezed my visits into the nooks and crannies of each day."

Some principals work to schedule a block or two per day for observation and ask that they not be disturbed during these sacred times. There are a couple of things related to this method that interfere with success. One is that issues arise because a principal often ends up being called away anyway. The other relates to the goals of seeing teachers in the beginning, middle, and end of class and in each course that a teacher teaches over the school year. Prescheduled blocks don't always allow for the freedom necessary to do all of these visits. So, using small blocks of time is one of the most effective methods to help get all the visits done.

Question All Clerical Responsibilities

It is important for principals to take inventory of their responsibilities to determine the ones that are more clerical in nature. Of those clerical tasks, which can be handed off to administrative assistants? Make a list. Examples include weekly staff memos, common disciplinary e-mails, or letters to parents. These can at least be partially done by assistants once a template has been created. Principals come in at the end and fine-tune or add the personalized bit instead of doing the whole thing. Delegating as many clerical duties as possible to administrative assistants has proven to be the most effective way to create time.

Rethink E-Mail

Don't let e-mails (answering or writing them) eat valuable time during the day. E-mail has this strange power to suck people in, and suddenly massive amounts of time that could be spent visiting classes are lost. There is no doubt that the volume of e-mails that principals receive is overwhelming, resulting in a desire to minimize the size of one's in-box.

However, what if the way principals handled e-mail was entirely different? What if principals had their administrative assistants handle their e-
mails? That doesn't mean every e-mail. However, if they went through e-
mails and responded to the ones they could, which is a lot, and told you
which ones required specific responses from principals, enormous amounts
of time could be saved. Assistants answer e-mails, schedule meetings for e-
mails that require it, and protect the principal's time. Administrative assistants and principals meet each day to share e-mail and meeting details. This
time spent on the back end saves much time on the front end. E-mail then
becomes a manageable activity that doesn't interfere with doing visits.

Manage Meetings

Have your administrative assistants manage your meetings. All scheduling
goes through them. They schedule all of them for short ten- to twenty-minute
blocks of time and interrupt you if they go long. It saves you loads of time.

No Emergencies

There are "emergencies" seemingly every day. How many are really emergencies requiring attention that minute? Not many. Make administrative assistants the gatekeepers of emergencies. Instruct faculty to contact administrative assistants with urgent problems. The assistants will judge the urgency
and almost always protect the principal's time.

Play to Strengths

Ideally, all principals and assistant principals spend time observing teachers
equally with everyone doing twenty-four combined visits per week. The
reality in some schools is that the volume of behavior issues prevents everyone from doing all the visits. In these situations, play to your strengths. If one
administrator, no matter the title, is better at discipline and another is more
warm and fuzzy and easily builds teacher relationships, then divide the duties
accordingly.

Prioritize Creating a Daily Schedule of Visits

Make creating the schedule of visits the first responsibility of the day. Doing
so creates time by helping principals know which periods are most likely to
be used for observations or reflective conversations. Knowing which blocks
of time are most likely to be spent in class allows principals to better organize the rest of the day.

Start Strong

Starting the day strong is a powerful way to create time. Getting at least one visit (preferable two) done in the first period makes it much easier to find time for the rest of the visits.

Five Minutes

Every day, there are numerous tiny increments of available time in the five-minute range. It can be difficult to know what to do productively during these mini-slots. Using them to do anything on a to-do list saves a lot of time over the course of the day. Answer an e-mail. Start a draft of a letter. Pop in on a teacher to answer a question. Using these increments buys you time.

Don't E-Mail Feedback

Sometimes, administrators feel they can save time by e-mailing feedback instead of meeting with teachers directly. Avoid this temptation at all costs. Always meet with teachers. E-mailing feedback instead of meeting them is never okay. TBO is built on the premise that teachers take risks when they have safe, trusting relationships with their principals. E-mailing feedback erodes trust rapidly. Teachers read feedback, and because there is no tone conveyed in the messages, they worry and wonder, creating fear and destroying trust. Any time that is saved by this act of e-mailing feedback interferes with the growth of teaching and is therefore not worth the time.

Be a Manager or Instructional Leader

There will always be managerial duties that accompany the job. Principals could logically and fairly suggest that the volume of these duties is so great that they could legitimately spend the entire day at their desks tending to them. Although this is true, where is the impact with this approach? Why did you become a principal? Hopefully, to make a difference in the lives of young people. The best way to help students is by helping teachers get better. Prioritize visiting classes. Some of those managerial duties aren't a necessity. Proudly wearing the instructional leader hat helps to prioritize the time necessary to do the visits, and it builds the respect and admiration of teachers as well.

ORGANIZATION TOOLS

There is also organization to be done to facilitate the smooth functioning of TBO. Possessing the proper tools helps principals be and stay organized, allowing for greater focus when doing visits. The organizational tools to be created before beginning implementation include the following:

- Observation folder
- Master schedule
- Teacher observation spreadsheet
- Teacher folders
- "Notes" documents

Beginning with the observation folder and working through the rest of these documents, a brief description is shared here, and in some cases, the how-to and reasoning for the documents are provided. As you read through these descriptions, remember that one of the keys to creating the time necessary for the continuous cycle of visits is using support mechanisms to lighten the load. Therefore, observers are encouraged to begin implementing their new time creation skills by using their administrative assistants' superior clerical skills to create the tools. TBO recommends using Google products to create them because of their easy shareability. After each reflective conversation, observers share a viewable copy of the observation form with the teacher. Google Docs makes this task a seamless process.

Observation Folder

The simple act of creating an electronic observation folder to house all observation-related documents allows all teacher observations and other necessary forms, documents, and tools to be stored and easily accessed in one place.

Master Schedule

Having an easily accessible and viewable cumulative schedule of all teachers' prep and teaching periods facilitates the quick creation of the daily schedule of visits.

Teacher Observation Spreadsheet

Having a spreadsheet to track observation visits and reflective conversations is crucial to managing the cycle of visits. This tool allows observers to systematically mark visits while working continuously from department to department.

As far as the how-to, create a separate sheet for each academic department. Occasionally, there is a teacher who teaches in more than one department. In those instances, list them and all their courses in one department; it's easier to manage their visits this way. It's pretty simple to set everything else up. On each sheet in the left-hand column, list the teachers in each

Teacher Observation Spreadsheet Sample

Teacher	Sept	Oct	Nov	Dec	T&L Align
Erin					
Math 6	28 M			10 B	May C=Y A=Y
PreAlg 7	5 M/E	13 M	8 M		Oct C=Y A=Y
Fabi					
IB 11HL				11 B	Apr C=Y A=Y
IB 12HL	12 M	18 M			Sept C=Y A=Y
Ed					
Alg 8				15 M	Mar C=Y A=Y
Alg 10	12 B	13 M	8 M		Nov C=N A=N
Cristine					
IB 11HL				15 B	May C=Y A=Y
IB 11SL	12 B				Sept C=Y A=Y
IB 12SL		17 M	10 E		
Maria					
Geo 9			8 M	10 B	Nov C=Y A=Y
Studies 11	13 B				Apr C=Y A=Y
Studies 12		17 M/E			

department followed by the courses they teach. On the top row, list the months of the school year and create two extra columns for the two special accountability reflective conversation visits (discussed later). It's that simple.

To use the spreadsheet to track visits, on a daily basis as observations are being done, write the number of that day of the month and either B, M, or E for beginning, middle, or end in the corresponding box. When the reflective conversation takes place, highlight the box to indicate completion of that cycle.

As observers can see, sometimes an observation covers two periods of class: beginning and middle or middle and end. In those cases, write two letters in the box. The goal is to see each course a teacher teaches and see the teacher in action during the beginning, middle, and end of class. It's worth noting that getting in to do observations at the beginning of the class is challenging; therefore, observers are advised to be cognizant of this difficulty and make extra efforts to get in to the crucial start of class.

Teacher Folders

Within the observation folder, create an individual folder for each teacher in order to house completed observation forms, teaching and learning alignment documents, and their individual "notes" document in an organized fashion.

Notes Documents

Within each teacher's folder, create a notes document to write notes or comments that for various reasons observers do not want on the observation forms. Remember that an initial focus of the reflective conversations is building relationships by noticing teaching strengths. To foster this relationship, it's best to not include improvement suggestions on the observation form initially. Also, when it is time to work on growth areas, teachers perform best when their focus is concentrated on one area at a time. So, examples of using the document are to write areas for growth as separate notes for later use. To use the notes document most effectively, observers are encouraged to date the notes and always write the newest notes on top. There are three other crucial forms to be housed in the observations folder:

- Trust-based observation/reflection form
- Today's visits
- Teaching and learning alignment

Trust-Based Observation/Reflection Form

This form will be discussed in detail in the next chapter.

Today's Visits

The today's visits form is used to create the daily schedule of observations and reflective conversations. To use the scheduler, at the beginning of each day, write down the names of the next five or six teachers to be observed. Why five or six when there are only three teacher observations per day? Because frequently observers will enter a classroom and have something going on that prevents an effective observation. The class might not be there, or there might be a test, lengthy quiz, or film. By having extra teachers written down, observers already know whom to observe next. The extra minutes spent writing down the next teachers' schedules save time later.

For all observed teachers, write down the courses and periods they teach that day. When viewing the spreadsheet, it becomes apparent when a certain class hasn't been seen yet or a certain portion of teaching hasn't been observed. In those cases, highlight that class and note B, M, or E as a reminder of which part of class to observe. For reflective conversations, write these teachers' names down and their prep periods. Use these lists to prioritize visits.

Teaching and Learning Alignment

TBO has built in a mechanism to ensure alignment between intended teaching, course standards, and assessments. The teaching and learning alignment document is used to facilitate and document this important accountability piece. Once per semester, the timing of which is at the principal's discretion, observers extend the reflective conversation in order to check for three-way alignment between the learning targets witnessed in the lesson; the knowledge, understanding, and skills derived from course standards/benchmarks in that unit's curricular plans; and the summative assessment for that unit.

To accomplish this task, at the completion of the reflective conversation, have teachers open their unit plans and summative assessments. As observers, it will be fairly easy to have teachers show direct alignment between learning targets and skills, knowledge, or understandings and associated standards/benchmarks in the unit plan. It will be equally easy, assuming that the connection has been made, for teachers to show alignment between intended teaching of the lesson's learning targets and either questions or a project element in the summative assessment.

It's important that teachers are teaching and testing the right things. This twice-per-year check allows observers to quickly check for alignment. An added bonus is that these checks send a message to teachers about the expectation that these connections are in place.

On the document, put an X if teachers can demonstrate alignment. For further documentary evidence, depending on district requirements, observers can list learning targets and the specific knowledge, skills, and/or understandings, specific standards/benchmarks, and specific questions or problems/projects that align with the summative assessment.

Part 3

The Observation

Chapter Five

Trust-Based Observation Form

Origins and Development

Actually, when TBO began, there was no form. Originally, the observations were scripted, writing the words of both teacher and students on a laptop. Through this combination of scripting and frequent visits, it was fairly easy to see and write about important elements of the teaching and the lesson. Over time, it was possible to gain the following:

- A sense of the teaching and personality of each teacher
- A sense of all the courses each teacher taught
- The personalities of different groups of students
- A picture of what the learning looked like in different classes
- A sense of the strengths and potential growth areas for each teacher

Despite the early success, administrators on multiple occasions encouraged less reliance on scripting. They wanted something that clearly articulated and looked for specific effective pedagogical practices. The suggestion was to either use a Danielson- or a Marzano-type rubric or to create a form listing good pedagogical practices.

One administrator asked a good question: "How do you specifically know what good teaching is?" With experience, it's pretty easy to feel you know what good teaching practices are, to know good teaching when you see it, and to trust your gut instincts to guide you on what to write down or what to talk about later with teachers. At the same time, admittedly, there are advantages to having designated "look-fors" and, more important, areas of practice to point teachers toward in order to improve.

In hindsight, the bigger concern was that using a rubric with pedagogy lists meant grading or rating teachers, which would interfere with the reflective growth conversations. Teachers wouldn't trust as much and therefore wouldn't be as open or willing to try new things. So, not surprisingly, there was resistance to the suggestions. The power of scripting as part of the model had been felt firsthand. Teachers had made incredible growth strides in their practice, improvements that felt like a direct result of the model.

For example, one teacher who was a heck of a nice guy had good relationships with students and amazing content knowledge, but his teaching was very lecture-heavy. His students' Advanced Placement scores were not strong, too many two and ones (on a five-point scale). Because of the development of a trusting relationship, he was open to constructive suggestions on ways to get better. There was agreement that working on adding cooperative learning to his teaching would help with student engagement, critical thinking, and retention of knowledge. Arrangements were made for him to take a Kagan Cooperative Learning workshop and to work with another teacher in the building who was very strong at cooperative learning.

The next year, his students' Advanced Placement scores were raised by more than a point on average. Absolutely amazing! The subsequent year, he even started coleading professional development workshops on cooperative learning—all because the model allowed for a trusting relationship to be built, a relationship such that he embraced the risk taking involved to completely reimagine his teaching practice.

There had also been the wonderful experiences when teachers were made aware of some innate skill they used, a skill they were completely unaware of until they saw the script of what they had said. Gwen's story is a perfect example of this scripting power.

Gwen was a very strong math teacher. She explained things clearly, frequently worked with kids individually in class, and formatively assessed nearly constantly during the course of a class. Gwen knew that she did these things. The thing Gwen didn't know that she did was empower her students by constantly encouraging and praising their efforts and successes. She would give it an "Atta boy," a "You got this," or a "Keep going, keep working on this. You'll get it," and many more as she worked her way around the room checking in with her students and offering support. You couldn't help but notice the frequency of her comments and the positive effect it seemed to have on her students. When this skill was shared with her, she looked baffled. She was completely oblivious to how and the frequency with which she encouraged her students. Scripting was instrumental in getting her to realize this strength. She was shocked and then pleased and proud when quote after quote of her words of encouragement to her students were read to her.

After these and other successes, the thought of changing a successful practice was not appealing, especially knowing that grading teachers would undermine the core of the success: trusting relationships. However, things soon changed after more "encouragement," which meant an administrator saying, "There is no evidence that backs up scripting as an effective method of observing, so it's time to change it!"—thus began the creation of what is now the trust-based observation form.

The hope was that a middle ground could be developed. Scripting does bring value, and there are research-proven pedagogical strategies that are an effective part of teaching practice. The only absolute was that there had to be no evaluative grading of teachers.

As work began, there was a keen awareness from personal experience, both as a teacher and as a principal, that models of evaluation seemed enormous. There were so many areas to observe that the templates felt unwieldy, unmanageable, and overwhelming. Evidence backed this belief, a suggestion for the development of shorter observation rubrics that focus on the most essential parts of a lesson. TNTP, a nonprofit organization dedicated to ending educational inequality, added, "Any rubric with more than 10 scored elements is likely to see significant covariation among the standards . . . beyond a handful of indicators, observers have too much trouble keeping the competencies and indicators distinct and become overloaded" (TNTP 2013). They concluded by writing,

> It's clear that bigger is not better. Rubrics do not need to be comprehensive frameworks that describe each element of successful teaching practice, nor should they include every possible technique a teacher could use inside or outside the classroom. Such bloated forms with excessive numbers of indicators lead to wasted effort by observers without adding precision. . . . An observer's time is better spent focusing on a small number of essential components of a successful lesson . . . so they can spend more time composing feedback that will support teacher development . . . put observation rubrics on a diet. (TNTP 2013)

Having had encounters with these bloated models, that feeling of paralysis, looking for each pedagogical area, is real. It often felt like the meat of the teaching was missed because of the struggle to notice *all* the pedagogical strategies.

Kim Marshall's experience was similar, writing that "trying to keep track of items on detailed instruments or rubrics makes it much more difficult to be a thoughtful and perceptive observer. The more detailed and elaborate the checklist, the more consumed the principal is with recording data, the less perceptive at observing what's going on, the more superficial the observations, and the less seriously the teacher will take the feedback" (Marshall 2013). Armed with these data, a decision was made to make the form as manageable as possible and limit the number of pedagogical strategies to no more than ten. Does that mean effective strategies are being left out? Yes, of course, and what a great trade in exchange for manageability and effectiveness!

So with experience and research guiding decisions, the form was created and altered multiple times to include the "Evidence of" areas listed on the form.

Trust Based Observation/Reflection Form

Teacher Name: **Subject:**

1) **What were you doing to help students learn? (Pedagogical tools)**
2) **If you had the opportunity to re-teach the entire lesson what, if anything, might you have done differently?**
3) **Question of the Year.**
4) **What progress have you made on your Action Research Big Goal?**
5) **Is there anything specific you would like me to look for on the next visit? Or anything you would like me to add about this visit?**

EVIDENCE OF:
LEARNING TARGET (Toolbox Possibilities: Rubrics; Exemplars):

Areas of Observation:	"X" if observed
"I statement," using active verb, specific to skill, knowledge or understanding and written in developmentally appropriate student language	
Unpacked at beginning of class	
Constantly displayed during class	
Use of rubrics/exemplars connected to LT	
Use of performance of understanding	
Formatively assessed during class	
Reviewed at end of class	

RISK TAKING/INNOVATIVE PRACTICE:

TEACHER/STUDENT RAPPORT and RELATIONSHIP (Toolbox Possibilities: Personal Discourse/1-on-1; Tone; Humor; Respect; T Sharing of Themselves; T Sharing Mistakes; Empathy; Knowledge of Ind St; Body Language; Relentlessness; Accountability; High Expectations; Feedback to Students; Active Listening; Use of Praise):

CLASSROOM and STUDENT BEHAVIOR MANAGEMENT (Toolbox Possibilities: Enforceable Statements; Choices; Empathy; L&L Strategies; Strong Class Beginnings; 10:2; Proximity Control; Strong Transitions; Responsive Teaching; Restorative Practice; Feedback--Specific and Timely; Cooperative Learning; With-it-ness; Interventions; Group Contingencies; Tangible Recognition; Clear Expectations; Consequences):

COOPERATIVE LEARNING (Toolbox Possibilities: Kagan Cooperative Learning Structures; PIES (Individual Accountability, Equal Participation); Room Set-Up; Role Assignments):

Structure Activity	P-Positive Interdependence	I-Individual Accountability	E-Equal Participation	S-Simultaneous Interaction

WORKING MEMORY: 10/2/REFLECTION AND PROCESSING TIME (Toolbox Possibilities: 10:2; Chunk and Chew' Kagan Structure; 3,2,1; 1 question; Drawing; Text Message/Twitter Post; 1 Minute Paper; Sample Test Questions; 6 Words; One Sentence/Paragraph Summary; Dear Absent Student; Whiteboards; $2/Headline Summary, Analogy):

Time	Activity	Time	Reflection Activity

QUESTIONING/HIGHER ORDER THINKING (Toolbox Possibilities: Bloom's Revised Checklist):

GOOD QUESTIONS AND BLOOM'S REVISED TAXONOMY	THINK TIME	HOW MANY ANSWER	QUESTION SPECIFICS

From Francis (2016, 2018).

FORMATIVE ASSESSMENT/KNOWING WHAT EACH STUDENT HAS LEARNED TO GUIDE NEXT STEPS (Toolbox Possibilities: Interviews; Conferring; 10:2/Chunk 'n Chew; Cooperative Learning; Questioning; Note Taking; Graphic Organizers; Exit Slips; Rubrics; Exemplars; Demonstration Station; Examples/Non-examples; Mini-Whiteboards; 10, 50 100 Word Summary; 3 Things; Analogy; Metacognition Exit; Back Channel; Draw It; 1 Minute; Online Quiz; Plickers; Photo Capture; New Clothes; Do's & Don'ts; Yes/No chart; Explain What Matters; Venn Diagram; Non-graded Quizzes Self and Peer Assessment)

WHO: TEACHER PEER-TO-PEER STUDENT	HOW: IN THE MOMENT PLANNED FOR EMBEDDED	TYPE: OBSERVATIONS CONVERSATIONS ARTIFACTS OF LEARNING	ASSESSMENT SPECIFICS

DESCRIPTIVE PROGRESS FEEDBACK (Toolbox Possibilities: Modeling; Peer Coaching; Self Coaching; Rubrics; Exemplars; Conferring; Met, Not Yet Met; I Noticed; More of, Less of; What's Working?, What's Not?, What's Next?; Highlighters; Traffic Lights; Post It Notes; Two Stars and a Wish; Margins; But What if You Did?):

WHO: TEACHER INFORMAL TEACHER FORMAL PEER-TO-PEER SELF	TYPE: BASIC INSTRUCTIONAL COACHING	FEEDBACK SPECIFICS

SPECIFIC DIFFERENTIATION: (**Toolbox Possibilities:** Flexible Grouping; Tiering; Graphic Organizers; Centers; Learning Contracts/Agendas; Small Group Instructions; Enrichment/Extensions; Think Dots/Task Cards/Think Tac Toe/Menus; Project/Problem/Performance Based Learning; RAFT; Remediation/Extension Activities; Multimedia/Technology; Conferring; Cooperative Learning; Rubrics; Chunk 'n Chew; Learner Preference Cards; Learner Profile Quick Surveys; Compacting; Anchor Activities)

METHOD: INTUITIVE INTENTIONAL	AREA: CONTENT PROCESS PRODUCT	LEARNER VOICE and ACCESS: READINESS INTEREST LEARNER PREFERENCE	DIFFERENTIATION SPECIFICS

LEARNING PRINCIPLES USED:

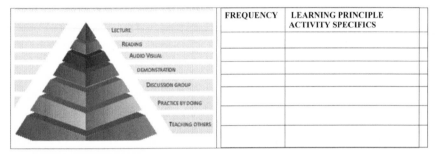

		FREQUENCY	LEARNING PRINCIPLE ACTIVITY SPECIFICS
LECTURE			
READING			
AUDIO VISUAL			
DEMONSTRATION			
DISCUSSION GROUP			
PRACTICE BY DOING			
TEACHING OTHERS			

STUDENT INTERVIEW: IS LEARNING CLEAR TO ALL?
Can students articulate what their learning target is and why it has value (extension/further use in life)?
Can students demonstrate learning of their target, the how they know they have learned it?

TEACHING INTANGIBLES, SCRIPTING, QUESTIONS, SUGGESTIONS, and ADDITIONAL PEDAGOGY:

Trust-Based Observation & Reflection Form.

The first thing you might notice is that, at first glance, there are eleven listings, exceeding the self-imposed limit of ten. Looking further, though, two of the areas—Risk-Taking/Innovative Practice and Learning Principles—are not pedagogy. Both have value, and that's why they are on the form, and that value will be explained in the next chapter, but they are not additional look-fors to burden observers. The form can be further explained as follows:

- The questions, explained in detail in an upcoming chapter, have been placed at the top of the form to serve as a reminder for observers to start the reflective conversations by asking the questions first before going over the observation itself.

- The term "Evidence of" is used to remind observers to look for the teaching strengths you notice, strengths that, when shared with teachers, build trusting relationships.
- "Toolbox Possibilities" and the accompanying Web links were added so that the form could double as a resource growth tool for both observers and teachers. This addition turned out to be useful for observers, guiding them on what to potentially look for and helping them to be more specific in writing down what they observe. The Web links for each tool have proven useful to teachers by providing immediate access to professional development reading and learning.
- The eight "Evidence of" documentation tables were added over time as experience and new learning provided understandings that the tables provided additional specificity that clarified teaching expectations and aided in growth.
- The student interview was added as a response to a flaw in the traditional observation process: what principals observe is whether teachers are *teaching*. The crucial question is whether students are *learning*. To answer that, we need some measure of learning (Dynarski 2016). Student answers to the interview questions have shown to be a solid measure of whether learning aligns with teaching and have been used effectively to guide talks on improving the alignment between the two.
- The last section: Teaching intangibles, scripting, questions, suggestions, and additional pedagogy have been added over time as a way to provide for a number of things:

  - Teaching intangibles provides a place to honor and comment on the less quantifiable art-of-teaching moments that observers notice.
  - Scripting provides a place to value and write crucial teacher words and moments.
  - Questions and suggestions provide a place to comment on wonderings outside the body of pedagogy notes. These notes were originally written inside each area, and that turned out to be problematic during reflective conversations. As soon as teachers heard the wondering, perceived as a negative, they tended to tune out other comments about observed strengths, which interfered with building relationship. Writing questions and suggestions here has eliminated that problem.
  - As stated earlier, the form limits pedagogy to nine items; additional pedagogy observed, in addition to those areas, can be written about and acknowledged here.

As a final side note to readers interested in adopting TBO, feel free to use the form in its entirety or to modify parts to suit your own beliefs, which might place a higher priority on some pedagogy areas that the TBO form doesn't address. The important things to remember are the following:

- Make sure the form is manageable in length. Don't add to the form; instead, swap something out to keep the form to ten or fewer categories.
- Ask the questions first.
- Focus on observed teaching strengths in the evidence of sections.
- Remember that growth, risk taking, and innovation happen when a trusting relationship is established between teachers and observers.

Chapter Six

Starting an Observation

You have your schedule for the day, and it's time to get started. As a reminder, if it's Monday through Thursday, the schedule lists the courses and class periods for the three teachers you are planning on observing plus the two or three backup teachers in case any of those teachers are not available. If it's Tuesday through Friday, your schedule lists the prep periods of the teachers you observed the day before.

Armed with your schedule, before you walk into class to do an observation, you want the following documents open on your laptop:

- Observation tracking spreadsheet
- Trust-based observation/reflection form (see the previous chapter)
- The file folders for the teachers you are planning on observing that day
- The notes document for the teachers you are planning on observing that day

When you walk into a class, find a seat and do the following:

1. Go to the observation tracking spreadsheet, find that teacher, and in the correct column and row write the date by number (e.g., 9 for the 9th and B, M, or E for the beginning, middle, or end portion of the class period you are observing).
2. Open the trust-based observation/reflection form, make a copy, and rename it by adding that teacher's name and today's date. Be sure to also house the new document in that teacher's observation folder.
3. In the new document, type the teacher's name and the subject being observed in the appropriate areas at the top of the form.

Table 6.1.   Trust Based Observation/Reflection Form

Teacher Name:	Subject:

1. What were you doing to help students learn? (pedagogical tools)

Now you're ready to observe. As you begin, make initial notes in these three areas:

- Working memory
- Learning target
- Learning principles

Begin with working memory and write the time and your best brief description of the current activity in the first two columns, unless it's obvious that you are watching a reflection/processing activity. In those instances, write it in the last two columns. Writing the time, as a bonus, also provides the start time for your twenty-minute observation (see table 6.1). Do the following for the learning target, no matter when you enter the class:

- Look to see if the learning target (LT) is displayed. If it is, type X in the corresponding column.
- Is an "I statement," using an active verb and specific to skill, knowledge, or understanding and written in developmentally appropriate student language, present? If it is, type X the corresponding column. (See table 6.2.)

Do the following for learning principles:

- Type a 1 in the frequency column, which aligns with the activity you are observing.
- Briefly write a description of the current class activity in the second column (see figure 6.1).

Table 6.2.

Time	Activity	Time	Reflection Activity
9:14	Cooperative Learning		

Table 6.3.

Areas of Observation	X if Observed
"I" statement, using active verb, specific to skill, knowledge, or understanding and written in developmentally appropriate student language	
Unpacked at beginning of class	
Constantly displayed during class	
Use of rubrics/exemplars connected to LT	
Use of performance of understanding	
Formatively assessed during class	
Reviewed at end of class	

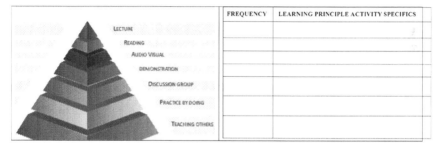

Figure 6.1.

Congratulations—you have started your observation. Now you are ready to get into the meat of observing: looking at teaching and learning. Use the form, your eyes, your ears, your gut instinct, and the information in the next chapter to guide you on what to write and mark. Make sure to take the time to interview at least one student during the course of the observation to ensure that intended teaching to the learning target matches actual student learning.

Chapter Seven

Evidence Of . . .

How do we get others to change? In reality, you can't make anyone change; people only change themselves. What you can do is create the conditions where change is more likely to happen. As a leader, you create those conditions by taking a strengths-based approach for learning and leadership and unleashing talent in your organization. —George Couros

As you know, TBO is about building trusting relationships with teachers so that they feel comfortable taking risks in order to improve teaching and learning. The "Evidence of" section of the form is the beginning piece in building those relationships. In looking for evidence, you are documenting varying degrees of teaching strengths. In doing so, observing becomes the beginning of the strengths-based approach described by Couros (2015) in *The Innovator's Mindset*. Later, during reflective conversations, you build the foundation of a trusting relationship as you share those observed strengths with teachers. This chapter guides you through general thoughts on observing successfully as well as each of the specific "Evidence of" areas.

EARLY THOUGHTS TO GUIDE SUCCESSFUL OBSERVATIONS

Before sharing how to conduct observations, it is important to touch again on the idea of rating teacher pedagogy. Assigning developmental ratings of observed practice could potentially tell teachers where they are in relation to innovative or leading practice in any pedagogical area. Research shows, however, that evaluatively grading pedagogy works against building trusting relationships and therefore growth. To ease the minds of those worrying about eliminating ratings, remember that TBO provides ratings rubrics for pedagogy. At the right time, during reflective conversations, principals will work with teachers using their pedagogical self-assessment rubric ratings to support their teaching improvement.

The "Evidence of" section is about pedagogy and helps you get to know your teachers, their strengths, and their areas for growth. As you move forward, remember that "Evidence of" is for writing down observed good practice in a particular area. The "Toolbox Possibilities" in each category work as a guide to help you to be semantically specific when writing the teaching and learning strategies you observe.

To be clear, because "Evidence of" is for writing strengths, this doesn't mean you don't make notes on or offer suggestions for growth. It means that notes on areas for improvement aren't written in "Evidence of." Notes on improvement written here are perceived as criticisms and interfere with trust building during the reflective conversation. Write down notes on areas for growth or improvement in the individual notes document you have for each teacher or in the suggestions area on the form.

As discussed earlier, the form has been kept to nine manageable areas to look for during an observation. Will you ever find all nine in one visit? Not likely. Does it matter? Not in the least. The absence of evidence in any category means nothing by itself in a single observation or even in multiple ones. TBO visits are frequent, and the accumulation of visits over time provides the overall picture of that teacher. Principals can easily be tempted to write about the absence of some area of practice. Don't! It means nothing in isolation, and, depending on the area, it might not mean anything negative because a teacher may be so strong in so many other areas that it makes up for whatever this particular absence is.

Although the "Evidence of" section functions as an effective guide for valuable areas of good practice to look for, it is important to allow yourself to trust more than just the categories on the form. What do you find yourself noticing? What draws your attention? It matters. Write it down. Follow where your gut, your heart, your mind, and your eyes take you; trust that what you notice, see, and feel is important. You never know what you might discover.

The combination of trusting these sometimes less tangible perceptions and using the "Evidence of" categories as a helping guide creates the most effective observations. Just like teaching, observing is a combination of craft, skill, and art. By tapping into trusting your instincts and using the "Evidence of" categories, you become a well-rounded observer best positioned to help your teachers grow.

Another important reminder is that all observers bring biases based on individual experiences. Denying bias risks damaging relationships with teachers. To combat bias, analyze what you've written to be sure it isn't influenced by a prejudice that might impede the growth of a teacher. If you are confronted on a bias and it's accurate, then own it and be open to your own growth by listening to teacher perspectives that might vary from your own.

"Toolbox Possibilities" contain abridged but thorough lists of teaching strategies for teachers to use in each area. Having them on the form helps to serve as strategy reminders for teachers and observers alike, and they allow observers to more accurately describe what is going on in the classroom. As an observer, write the toolbox strategy you see followed by a few words on the specifics of what was observed. If it furthers evidence and is helpful, also write down specific quotes of what teachers say. The power of using teachers' actual words cannot be overstated.

Most people won't be familiar with *all* the toolbox strategies. That is to be expected, but learning as many as possible does help with observations and coaching. When unsure or when guiding a teacher on improvement, obtain the details of a strategy by clicking on "Toolbox Possibilities" on the online form for that area to access educational articles on each topic.

Finally, observers will notice that some pedagogical strategies are listed in more than one toolbox area on the form. Those strategies effectively serve multiple purposes and therefore are listed in all appropriate areas.

As the details of each "Evidence of" area are explained, it will be helpful to understand the writing format. Each section begins with an explanation of the *rationale* for having that area on the form, including evidence supporting its value. Next is advice on *completing this section*, which provides the nuts and bolts of what to look for and write in that particular category. Lastly, *final thoughts* pertinent to that category are shared with readers. As you read the relevant categories, refer to the specified tables to add a visual guide.

LEARNING TARGETS

Rationale

Learning targets (LTs) describe, in language that students understand, the lesson-size chunk of information, skills, and reasoning processes that students will come to know deeply. We write LTs from the students' points of view and share them throughout today's lesson so that students can use them to guide their own learning (Moss and Brookhart 2012). They also convey to students the destination for the lesson—what to learn, how deeply to learn it, and exactly how to demonstrate their new learning (Moss and Brookhart 2009). They are concrete goals that clearly describe what students will learn and be able to do by the end of a class, unit, project, or even course. They begin with an "I can" statement and are posted in the classroom (Berger et al. 2014).

Using LTs improves outcomes because students learn more when they know what they are supposed to learn. Evidence backs it up: students who can identify what they are learning significantly outscore those who cannot (Marzano, as cited by Chappuis 2005). LTs provide a clear direction and result in meaningful learning and increased student achievement (Moss and Brookhart 2012).

LTs also boost student self-efficacy. When students use them, they are better able to compare where they are with where they need to go, set specific goals for what they will accomplish, choose effective strategies to achieve those goals, and assess and adjust what they are doing to get there as they are doing it. These factors boost their motivation to learn as they progressively see themselves as more confident and competent learners (Moss and Brookhart 2012).

Completing This Section

For the LT "Evidence of" area only, the criteria are subdivided and explained separately, addressing the look-fors and nuts and bolts of each element that make up the comprehensive picture of LTs (see table 7.1).

"I" Statement, Using Active Verb, Specific to Skill, Knowledge or Understanding and Written in Developmentally Appropriate Student Language

As an observer, make sure that LTs are written using "I" statements and active verbs. Make sure they are written at a level developmentally appropriate to the age of the students.

Sometimes there can be a tendency for teachers to write the LTs in the more teacher-friendly wording of standards or benchmarks; check for this tendency. Make sure the target or targets are in fact addressing a knowledge, skill, or understanding connected to the intended learning. Some teachers will have a tendency early on in their use of LTs to write an activity, not an LT. Watch for this common mistake. Observers will find that they quickly

Table 7.1.   Learning Target (Toolbox Possibilities: Rubrics; Exemplars)

Areas of Observation	X if Observed
"I" statement, using active verb, specific to skill, knowledge, or understanding and written in developmentally appropriate student language	
Unpacked at beginning of class	
Constantly displayed during class	
Use of rubrics/exemplars connected to LT	
Use of performance of understanding	
Formatively assessed during class	
Reviewed at end of class	

gain the ability to almost instantly notice if all of these expectations are there. When you see evidence of all the criteria, mark an X in this line of the table.

Unpacked at the Beginning of Class

When teachers unpack the LT well, they explain the target clearly enough that students understand the learning goal, know what good work on the assignment looks like (Moss and Brookhart 2009), know how to reach the goal, and understand and are able to articulate where their performance is in relation to mastering the target. After unpacking the target, students should have a clear picture of what meeting the target looks like, and they should have clarity on how their work time will lead them toward meeting the target (Berger et al. 2014).

So, as an observer, listen to make sure that the description of the target specifies what achieving the learning would look like and how students would know if they got it. Ask yourself if the description appears to make sense to the students. Look to see if the teacher reviews relevant vocabulary and has students focus on the active verb in the target. Look to see that the teacher explains to students how they will show that they have mastered the target, whether through class work or an assessment for learning at the end of the lesson (Berger et al. 2014).

You will be able to best gauge whether the targets are unpacked when you are there at the beginning of the class. Be aware, especially when you are not there for the beginning, that the student interview also allows you to gauge whether the targets were unpacked well. Evidence of unpacking that meets the descriptors just described, through either observation or students' answers to interview questions, allows you to mark an X in the second line of the table.

Constantly Displayed during Class

Students do a better job of keeping their eyes on the prize when they are regularly reminded of it. Having the target written where it is constantly visible to students allows for these regular visible reminders. So, as an observer, check that the LT is constantly visible and easy to notice. When you see that the LT is constantly visible, whether on the whiteboard or projected onto a screen, mark an X in the third line of the table.

Use of Rubrics/Exemplars Connected to LTs

Rubrics and exemplars are listed together in the table because they are so closely linked. Rubrics set the stage for knowing what is specifically to be learned and what different levels of success look like. Exemplars of different levels of the work of previous students guides current students toward knowing the quality of their work on the path toward the LT. Both play a valuable role in helping students reach an LT.

Success criteria answer an important question about the lesson from the student's point of view: "How will I know when I hit my learning target?" Students who examine examples of work against criteria in a rubric will be better able to assess their own performances. They will develop a more nuanced view of what quality work looks like for today's lesson and use that knowledge during the performance of understanding (Moss and Brookhart 2009).

So, as an observer, look for evidence that rubrics are being used and that the criterion for success is clear, specific to the LT, easily understandable to students, observable, and measurable (Stinson 2012). Look for evidence that exemplars are being used and that examples with a variety of levels of accomplishment are being used, not just "A"-caliber work. When you see evidence of rubrics and/or exemplars being used and they include the described elements, mark an X in the fourth line of the table. Write the word "rubric" and/or "exemplar" on the line as well; it helps memories during the reflective conversation.

Use of Performance of Understanding

Any attempts at teaching and learning are limited without students being given the opportunity to put the learning into practice. Performances of understanding do just that. They are what students are making, saying, doing, or writing (Foresi Follow 2013) and demonstrate understanding of knowledge, skills, ideas, and concepts (Cerbin and Kopp 2004). Strong performances of understanding relate directly to the LTs, allow opportunities to demonstrate understanding (Perkins and Blythe 1994), and are rigorous and relevant (Foresi Follow 2013). They help students try on the LT, deepen their understanding of important concepts and skills, and make their thinking visible so that they can gather evidence of what they know and how well they know it (Moss and Brookhart 2012).

So, as an observer, look to see if students are given a performance of understanding as part of the lesson, then look for the connection between the activity and the LT. It is more likely that you'll see these performances during the middle or end rather than in the beginning of a lesson. Know that the student interviews can add clarity to the quality of the performance and the link between it and the LT. When you see evidence of a performance of understanding linked to the LT, mark an X in the fifth line of the table. The expectation is for some performance of understanding every lesson.

Formatively Assessed during Class

Formative assessment is discussed in great detail later in this chapter, so the definition and explanation here will be brief. For the purposes of the LT table, formative assessment is the intentional process of continuously and systematically gathering evidence of learning with the express goal of improving student achievement. These assessments are done when teachers take stock of where current students' work is in relation to the goal. It is an "instructional tool" that teachers "use while learning is occurring" and "an accountability tool to determine if learning has occurred" (National Education Association 2001).

So, as an observer, the expectation is that during the course of any lesson, you will see multiple examples of teachers formatively assessing the class, either as a whole, in small teams, or individually, in order to make determinations on the levels of progress students are making toward the LT. When you see formative assessments of any type happening to some degree, mark an X on the sixth line of the table.

Reviewed at the End of Class

"Reviewed at end of class" is about teachers providing closure to the learning and the lesson. Often, teachers get caught up in teaching and trying to fit in all the content before class ends. The bell rings, and students move on to the next class. A review is purposeful and planned. Teachers are expected to go over the LT and the learning that, it is hoped, took place that class period. It is the "bringing it all together" portion of a lesson, the closure, the "what's next," a final check for understanding or questions.

So, as an observer, ask yourself if the LT is reviewed at the end of class, usually in the form of a final reexplanation and check for understanding. As long as a review happens, you can mark an X on the seventh line of the table. Obviously, you won't be able to see the review when observing during the beginning or the middle part of the class. That's okay.

Reviewing the LT is important, and having it on the form sends a message that it is an expectation that reviews happen every day. You will likely notice that teachers tend to not be strong at doing reviews at first. It is part of the process and can be addressed during reflective conversation when the time is right.

Final Thoughts

When teachers give students a good idea of what the end goal looks like, the chances of student success grow immensely. Observers look for LTs because there is no more foundational activity for a school leader than making sure that there are clear LTs aligned to standards, that teachers understand them and teach to them, and that students understand them and reach for them (Moss and Brookhart 2009).

- The absence of an X is not a negative or a sure sign of a growth area for a teacher.
- The thought of looking for seven elements in LTs can seem like a lot to observe over the course of a twenty-minute observation, especially with the other "Evidence of" categories on the observation form. However, experience shows that noticing the elements is actually a quick and simple check that takes very little time.
- It is impossible to see all seven LT elements during a twenty-minute observation. Over time, though, as you watch classes at the beginning, in the middle, and at the end, you will develop a comprehensive picture of a teacher's effectiveness using LTs.

RISK TAKING/INNOVATIVE PRACTICE

Rationale

One of the foundational differences between TBO and other observation models is that with TBO, teachers take more risks in their practice. Risk taking/innovative practice is on the observation form for one reason: to serve as a reminder for observers to verbally encourage and support teacher risk taking during reflective conversations.

The belief in risk taking as an improvement dynamic is widespread, but it does not occur as frequently as desired. The biggest obstacle is fear: when teachers teach in fear, they take few risks (Neves 2014). If school leaders are to successfully move forward in supporting growth, they will have to take appropriate actions so that people feel safe taking risks (O'Leary 2014). If we want people to take risks, they have to know that we are there to catch them and support them. They also need to see us leading by example and taking risks in our own work. Innovation is needed both in our classrooms and in our leadership. As leaders, we must model the kind of innovation we want to see (Couros 2015). Neves (2014) found that as employees' perceived organizational support increased, so did their trust that the organization would be benevolent in case of failure. When people feel supported, they trust more and aren't as afraid to try something that could result in failure.

Completing This Section

Risk taking is on the form for mostly symbolic reasons that will be discussed in detail during the reflective conversation. As an observer, feel free to write a clear example of a teacher trying something new or innovative, but it's not something you have to actively look for during the observation. This section being left blank is the norm for most observations.

Final Thoughts

School leaders have an amazing opportunity through the use of TBO to help instill a growth, risk-taking mindset in an entire building of teachers, students, and leaders. Observers lead this effort to encourage and develop growth mindset risk takers when they remind teachers that risk taking, even when the result is failure, is embraced. Having risk taking on the form overtly reminds observers to send this message over and over again.

On Teacher–Student Rapport and Relationships and Classroom and Student Behavior Management

The next two "Evidence of" categories—teacher–student rapport and relationships and classroom and student behavior management—are obvious necessities in order for learning to take place in a successful classroom. Although many teachers possess excellent strengths in these areas, these are not to be overlooked or taken for granted. Without passion for making a difference in the lives of kids, developing appropriate levels of teacher–student rapport is unlikely to be reached. These categories are listed next to each other because there is often a direct connection between strong teacher–student rapport and relationships and the ability to create and manage a safe, secure, and organized classroom. Everyone knows that creating strong and trusting student–teacher relationships helps ease the work of managing a class.

TEACHER–STUDENT RAPPORT AND RELATIONSHIPS

Students don't care how much you know until they know how much you care.
—John Maxwell

Rationale

It doesn't matter whether it's principal–teacher or teacher–student relationships, they all matter, and they all possess the power to influence one way or another. Strong teacher–student relationships shape the way children think and act in school. When students have a strong relationship with their teacher, they are more likely to feel positive about class and about school in general. They are also more willing to have a go at hard work, to risk making mistakes, and to ask for help when they need it (Australian Society for Evidence Based Teaching 2020). Teachers who have created positive teacher–student relationships are more likely to have above-average effects on student achievement (Hattie 2008).

Importantly, when students were asked about their best teachers, the common attributes mentioned were teachers who built relationships with students, teachers who helped students to have different and better strategies or processes to learn the subject, and teachers who demonstrated a willingness to explain material and help students with their work (Hattie 2008). All these attributes are examples of strong teacher–student relationships. Striving to be that make-a-difference teacher with each student is the ideal goal.

To be clear, though, when talking about teacher–student relationships, the call is not for a flowery love of all children without accompanying pushes for rigor and accountability; care alone does nothing to help a child reach beyond perceived abilities. Instead, the suggestion is, as Hattie (2008) has suggested, that holding high standards without providing a warm environment is merely harsh. A warm environment without high standards lacks backbone. But creating a combination of high standards with a warm and supportive environment will benefit all students (Hattie 2008).

Completing This Section

As an observer, look for examples of teachers using the relationship "Toolbox Possibilities." Although the list is not exhaustive, examples of one-on-one interaction, empathy, tone of voice, humor, respect, teachers' sharing of themselves and their humanity, teachers' sharing of their own mistakes, examples of teacher knowledge of individual students, working the room, proximity, accountability, high expectations, relentlessness, and body language all serve as evidence of teacher–student rapport and relationships. Write the strategies used, clarifying notes, and teacher quotes to support evidence.

Final Thoughts

- Although individual examples of evidence of teacher–student relationships don't necessarily provide overall evidence of strong relationship skills, over time enough examples will give observers a picture of where teachers are in their development of relationships.
- As a reminder, the success of TBO demands that observers model the relationship skills they want to see their teachers have with their students. If you can't model good relationships, you will struggle to successfully implement TBO.
- Three of the relationship tools—accountability, high expectations, and relentlessness—might not have the traditional appearance of being strong relationship tools to some observers, but they definitely are. Assuming

that the tone stays respectful, all three tools show that a teacher cares enough to make sure that nothing less than the student's best is acceptable.

CLASSROOM AND STUDENT BEHAVIOR MANAGEMENT

Rationale

As any behavior taking place in a classroom that either supports or interferes with the capability and capacity of students to learn the tasks and skills required to achieve educationally (Hattie 2008), classroom management matters. Management is unique among the "Evidence of" categories. In the other categories, the use of the pedagogy improves teaching and learning. In classroom management, however, it's not so much what good classroom management does to improve learning as what poor classroom management does to inhibit learning. In fact, if a teacher cannot obtain students' cooperation and involve them in instructional activities, it is unlikely that effective teaching will take place: poor management wastes class time, reduces students' time on task, and detracts from the quality of the learning environment (Marzano et al. 2003). So the bottom line is that reducing disruptive behaviors needs to be a core competency of any successful teacher (Hattie 2008).

Completing This Section

So, as an observer, look for examples of the "Toolbox Possibilities" being used by teachers. Although the list is not exhaustive, certainly examples of with-it-ness, disciplinary interventions, group contingency strategies, tangible recognition, direct consequences, clear expectations, extinguishing disruptive behaviors, enforceable statements, choice, empathy, strong class beginnings, strong transitions, and proximity all serve as evidence of teachers managing their classes. Write down the tool that you see evidence of; it provides clarity in the reflective conversation. Also write any additional relevant notes related to use of the strategy and any specific teacher quotes that might illuminate the use or the effectiveness of the strategy.

Final Thoughts

- Some of the tools that factor into strong classroom management are listed in other sections. For example, strong relationships usually result in better-managed classrooms. Another example is the variety and challenge of seat work, which could be called "engagement" or "differentiation" and listed in one of those categories. Mark them in those categories when they occur and then discuss the connection to that tool with management during the reflective conversation.

- If during an observation there is a sense that an issue with classroom management relates to teacher preparedness, make your note either at the bottom of the form or in that teacher's separate notes document and discuss at the appropriate time.
- For management, one strategy that is highly effective is establishing expectations and rules for the class at the beginning of the year. Since it is impossible to visit all teachers in the first week, observers are encouraged to trust their judgment on how well teachers set early expectations when a class isn't visited the first week or two.

Engagement: Cooperative Learning and Working Memory

These two strategies are on the form and next to each other because they are two of the best engagement strategies out there. Research shows that engaging students in the learning process increases their attention and focus, motivates them to practice higher-level critical thinking skills, and promotes meaningful learning experiences. Instructors who adopt a student-centered approach to instruction increase opportunities for student engagement, which then helps everyone more successfully achieve the course learning objectives (Center for Teaching and Learning 2019). Cooperative learning and working memory work powerfully to help students achieve learning goals, and they are also backed by brain research data on ways in which people learn best. Both deepen knowledge, build skills, strengthen understanding, and boost rates of retention.

COOPERATIVE LEARNING

Rationale

Cooperative learning is a successful teaching strategy in which small teams, made up of students with different levels of ability, use a variety of learning activities to improve their understanding of a subject. Each member of a team is responsible not only for learning what is taught but also for helping teammates learn, thus creating an atmosphere of achievement (Balkcom 1992).

The most compelling argument for cooperative learning is that it actively engages students in learning. Each student has an opportunity to contribute in a small group and is more apt to claim ownership of the material (National Education Association 2002). Getting students to work with each other helps them achieve better results. The use of cooperative learning groups adds value to whole-class instruction and to individual work (Killian 2016).

The effect size of cooperative learning on academic achievement is substantial. Through metastudies, data say that, on average, a student scoring at the 50th percentile in a traditional classroom would be scoring at the 73rd percentile had they been taught via cooperative learning (Dotson 2001). And using Kagan's (2014) cooperative learning structures, the average positive effect size for Kagan was an average gain from the 50th to 82nd percentile.

A word of caution on cooperative learning: sometimes what people perceive to be cooperative learning is in fact group work. The two are not the same. For cooperative learning, the basic elements make up the "PIES" acronym:

> Positive interdependence—occurs when gains of individuals or teams are positively correlated.
>
> Individual accountability—occurs when all students in a group are held accountable for doing a share of the work and for mastery of the material to be learned.
>
> Equal participation—occurs when each member of the group is afforded equal shares of responsibility and input.
>
> Simultaneous interaction—occurs when class time is designed to allow many student interactions during the period (Dotson 2001).

In group learning, the results are not strong because the above elements are not in place. One of the clearest ways to explain the difference is through an explanation of two seemingly similar activities most readers are familiar with: think-pair-share and timed-pair-share. The names and rules for the activities seem similar.

In both activities, students are given a question or a problem, given time to think, and then given an opportunity to share with each other in response to the question. The difference is in the details, though. In think-pair-share, those are the only rules, but in timed-pair-share, there are rules that take into account the necessary cooperative learning elements described above. In timed-pair-share, there are specific times for each partner to take turns being the speaker and the listener. This ensures both individual accountability and equal participation. Often in think-pair-share, the conversation ends up being dominated by one person, extending the learning gap as opposed to shrinking it.

It is also important to note that in true cooperative learning, groups have already been established heterogeneously, with each group containing one high, one medium-high, one medium-low, and one low student. These groupings ensure that students of varying abilities will work with each other, enhancing the chances that if one student doesn't know the answer, the other will, and they can then coach the other. This scenario is perfect because teaching others is the highest form of retention of knowledge. Compare this scenario to the likelihood in think-pair-share that not all the groups are heterogeneously created and therefore that there will be at least some groups where nobody will know the answer, leaving those groups without the ability to make sure that everyone knows or understands.

Reading this information might cause people to be afraid to incorporate cooperative learning into the repertoire of your teachers. Don't be—cooperative learning is relatively easy to begin to incorporate into practice. A one- or two-hour training on Kagan basics would be enough to get started on the cooperative learning path.

Best of all, it works for any class at any grade level and does not require extra planning. Teachers love it, and so do students. Kagan Cooperative Learning Structures can't be recommended strongly enough. Go or send one of your assistants or one of your teachers to their five-day workshops. You will be thrilled that you did.

Completing the Section

As an observer, look for examples of the strategies being used by teachers. Although the list is not exhaustive, examples of the essential five basic cooperative learning structures that serve as evidence of cooperative learning use include rally robin, timed-pair-share, round robin, rally coach or stand up, hand up, and pair up, as well as heterogeneous grouping, room setup, and PIES. Write down the cooperative structure that you see used in the first column. Mark an X in all of the PIES that are present during the activity (see table 7.2).

Final Thoughts

One of the best things about cooperative learning is that it does so much more than improve academic learning:

- Meta-analysis shows that cooperation promotes greater support, more frequent use of higher-level reasoning strategies, and more accurate perspective taking than does competitive or individualistic efforts. Thus, the more cooperative learning experiences students are involved in, the more ma-

Table 7.2. Cooperative Learning

Structure Activity	P: Positive Interdependence	I: Individual Accountability	E: Equal Participation	S: Simultaneous Interaction

Toolbox Possibilities: Kagan Cooperative Learning Structures; PIES (Individual Accountability, Equal Participation); Room Setup; Role Assignments

ture their cognitive and moral decision making and the more they will tend to take other people's perspectives into account when making decisions (Johnson and Johnson 2018).

- Cooperative learning structures also serve as fantastic opportunities to improve social-emotional learning. Students are taught and regularly given opportunities to learn to interact successfully with others. In this era when the development of social-emotional intelligence and learning is so valued in conjunction with academic learning, it is always fantastic when two birds can be killed with one stone.

- Cooperative learning additionally serves as an excellent formative assessment tool. Through the use of cooperative learning structures, teachers are able to immediately see who is getting it and who isn't.

- Because of the high engagement levels in cooperative learning structures and the improved social skills that students demonstrate from using cooperative learning, classroom management problems decrease as well.

- Although no single tool is a panacea, if there is one, cooperative learning structures might be it.

WORKING MEMORY: 10-2/REFLECTION AND PROCESSING TIME

Rationale

If students don't remember what is taught, nothing is gained. There are real, scientifically valid, critical limitations to learning that educators must accept and overcome (McGowan 2015).

> To learn, brains must process information in working memory before permanent storage can occur in long-term memory. . . . Thus in order for a student to think about and learn information presented in courses, processing must take place in the brain's working memory. . . . By chunking information a student can go beyond simple memorization of facts and begin to understand more complex materials. . . . If we present too much new material too quickly or in an inefficient way, a student's working memory will "overload" and needed processing (and hence learning) cannot occur. The material will not be stored in the student's long-term memory and therefore cannot be retrieved and used in the future. However, by properly sequencing material we can use a student's long-term memory to circumvent the limitations of working memory. (Volk 2017)

So, to keep students engaged, you must win the battle for their attention every ten minutes (Medina 2014). That is really what working memory is about. In 10-2, sometimes called, 10-2-2 or Chunk 'n' Chew, the strategy is straightforward. A learning activity goes on for ten minutes and is followed by two minutes of processing/reflection time, often done collaboratively. During the processing time, the teacher circulates and provides feedback to students (Venuto 2015).

Completing the Sections

As an observer, first determine whether you are watching an activity or a reflection activity. In the appropriate column, write the time that the activity begins. When filling in the activity column, use the words from the learning principles pyramid to describe the activity. When filling in the reflection/ processing activity column, write the "Toolbox Possibilities" strategy that best describes what's going on. When the next activity begins, repeat the process.

As a special note for this category, experience shows that there are teachers who do limit the information shared with students to short bursts and also use short reflective/processing activities to better embed learning. More frequently, though, teachers will initially fall into one of two categories: the chunks of information shared with students are much longer than ten minutes, or the chunks of information are appropriately short but true reflective activities are missing. These teachers will tend to go from one chunk to another but miss out on the processing/reflection time (see table 7.3).

Final Thoughts

- The table is really valuable during the reflective conversation. Being able to read the times that activities commence and whether they are regular or reflection/processing activities immediately lets teachers be self-informed on how productive they are at incorporating working memory into their practice. The table does the talking. It basically forces teachers to self-reflect.

Table 7.3.   Working Memory: 10-2 Reflection and Processing Time

Time	Activity	Time	Reflection Activity

Toolbox Possibilities: 10-2; Chunk 'n' Chew Kagan Structure; 3, 2, 1; 1 Question; Drawing; Text Message/Twitter Post; 1 Minute Paper; Sample Test Questions; 6 Words; One Sentence/Paragraph Summary; Dear Absent Student; Whiteboards; $2/Headline Summary, Analogy

- Although 10-2 is the co-name of the "Evidence of" category, it is important to remember that ten minutes is a maximum time for fully developed learners, basically high school students. Four-year-olds have about half the working memory of high schoolers. So, the recommendation is for teachers to take into account the basic principles of cognitive development and cognitive psychology, adjusting the materials to the working memory capabilities of the learner (Cowan 2014), so probably half that time for four-year-olds and so on until students reach high school and can absorb about ten minutes of learning in working memory. A viable general alternative for younger students is 5-1.
- As an added bonus, use of the strategy often doubles as a formative assessment opportunity for teachers. The use of one pedagogical strategy leads to the use of another.
- Many cooperative learning structures work perfectly as processing/reflection activities.

QUESTIONING/HIGHER-ORDER THINKING

Rationale

Teachers ask hundreds of questions every day, and it is important that they use questioning techniques that challenge the thinking of all of their students (Burton 2010). Teachers ask questions to check for understanding, to create active engagement, and to review content. The cognitive level of these questions factors into improved student performance, as does providing sufficient think time before having students ask and answer questions in a cooperative learning format that empowers all students.

> Striving to use more higher-order questions provides numerous benefits to students. Higher-order questions put advanced cognitive demand on students. They encourage students to think beyond literal questions. . . . They promote critical thinking skills because these types of questions expect students to apply, analyze, synthesize, and evaluate information instead of simply recalling facts. . . . According to research, teachers who effectively use a variety of higher-order questions can overcome the brain's natural tendency to develop mental routines and patterns to limit information, which is called *neural pruning*. As a result, students' brains may become more open minded, which strengthens the brain. . . . Higher-order questions increase *neural branching*, the opposite of neural pruning. (Bogdanovich 2014)

Completing This Section

As an observer, for each question a teacher asks, first determine the level of question that was asked. The question starters on the pyramid help to determine the level. Next, write the question (or at least the start of the question) in the corresponding "Question Specifics" column. In the corresponding "Think Time" column, write the amount of time the teacher gave students before asking for answers. Ideally, write the number of seconds of wait time; however, if you don't know the time and there was at least three seconds of wait time, write "yes"; otherwise, write "none." Finally, in the "How Many Answer" column, write "all" if the question was asked so that each student could answer; otherwise, write the number of students who could answer. As Spencer Kagan (2011), author of the *Kagan Online Magazine*, writes, "Why call on just one when we can call on everyone?"

Also look for teacher redirecting and probing, especially to incorrect answers so that they can be discussed at the appropriate time with teachers.

Final Thoughts

- All levels of questions are fine; the amount of lower-level questions depends on the ages and developmental levels of students and sometimes the content of the lesson. Having said that, observers are looking, over time, to see teachers increase the levels of the questions being asked; the more higher-level questions asked, the better.
- The pyramid is an excellent tool. It helps teachers self-analyze their questions and provides teachers with starter guidance for their questions. The

QUESTIONING/HIGHER ORDER THINKING (**Toolbox Possibilities:** Bloom's Revised Checklist):

Completing the Observation Form. From Francis (2016, 2018).

table almost ends up functioning as a mini professional development session just through its presence on the form.

- It can be difficult on occasion to determine the level at which the question belongs. Do the best you can, and if you misplace the level of the question, it is not a big deal because it will be by no more than one area. The point is giving teachers a visual representation of the levels of questions that teachers ask over time.

- Special thanks to the author of *Now That's a Good Question!* (Erik M. Francis), who has graciously allowed TBO to use his excellent levels-of-questioning pyramid.

ON FORMATIVE ASSESSMENT, DESCRIPTIVE PROGRESS FEEDBACK, AND SPECIFIC DIFFERENTIATION SECTIONS

The next three "Evidence of" sections on the form are listed together because all are connected to one another. Formative assessment is the process of determining where each student is in relation to understanding the learning. The information gleaned from these assessments, ideally performed multiple times over the course of each lesson, guides teachers on the following:

- Specific descriptive progress feedback to give to students
- Steps that might be necessary to differentiate and/or revise current or future instruction

Formatively assessing students, both purposefully and informally, provides teachers with vital information related to students' learning. With this information, feedback can take the form of progress analysis discussions, questioning, or even a teacher decision to immediately reteach or revise instruction. Formatively assessing where each student is provides the necessary information to potentially differentiate instruction for the needs of individuals and/or groups. This differentiation can potentially take the form of remedial steps for struggling students or advanced activities for students who are picking things up quite easily.

Formative assessment, descriptive progress feedback, and specific differentiation are all linked in one way or another to just about every area on the observation form. Student progress is being formatively assessed in relation to LTs. Many tools to formatively assess include the use of cooperative learning and/or working memory activities that improve not only engagement but also classroom management. Questioning is another tool used not only in formative assessment but in the feedback process as well.

Often, feedback and differentiation involve personal conferring, which is a good way to improve the teacher–student relationship, as does the simple act of differentiating instruction to meet the needs of individual learners. Students know and appreciate this individualized effort—it builds relationships. One of the best things about the form is that everything connects. Improving skills in one area almost by necessity improves skills in multiple other areas.

FORMATIVE ASSESSMENT/KNOWING WHAT EACH STUDENT HAS LEARNED

Rationale

In some ways, formative assessment is the most vital element for teachers to incorporate into their practice because, through its effective use, teachers gain a sense of whether the students are learning what the teachers are teaching. In other words, is what I'm doing working? Are the kids getting it? As John McCarthy (2017), author of *So All Can Learn*, writes, "Tracking students' progress daily is critical for ensuring that they do not fall behind without being noticed."

> Formative assessment can have a transformational effect on teachers and teaching. In a very real way it flips a switch, shining a bright light on individual teaching decisions so that teachers can see clearly (and perhaps for the first time) the difference between the intent and the effect of their actions. Armed with this new perspective, teachers can take constructive action in their classrooms. They begin to collect and use strong evidence of exactly what works and exactly what does not work in their classrooms, with their students. And as they critically examine their own knowledge, practices, and working assumptions—during each day, during each lesson, and during each interaction with their students—they become inquiry-minded and keenly aware of exactly where they need to focus their change and improvement efforts in order to raise student achievement. (Moss and Brookhart 2009)

The evidence supporting the effectiveness of formative assessment as a tool to improve teaching and learning is overwhelming. Hattie, Marzano, and Fullan all speak to the powerful effect that formative assessment has on teaching and learning. Studies have demonstrated that assessment for learning rivals one-on-one tutoring in its effectiveness (Stiggins 2004). There have been few initiatives in education with such a strong body of evidence to support a claim to raise standards (Black and Wiliam 2005).

It's really not surprising that formative assessment works so well. What is surprising is how few U.S. teachers use the process (Popham 2013). It is worrisome because when students are not assessed or do not receive feedback, they are unsure about their performance and assume that they are doing just fine. They are unlikely to make mid-course corrections in their learning.

When teachers fail to plan instruction based on student performance, misconceptions are reinforced, errors go unaddressed, and gaps in knowledge persist. When this is the case, teachers remain oblivious to the lack of real learning their students are doing (Frey and Fisher 2011). For each student, the goal is alignment between what is being taught and what is being learned; effective use of formative assessment is key to making that a reality and TBO can help.

Completing This Section

Before moving forward, it is important to share information on who can assess, how the assessments can be done, and the types of assessments teachers can use:

1. Who is assessing? It doesn't have to be only the teacher doing the work. Peers can formatively assess one another's work, and students can self-assess as long as teachers see the results.
2. How is the assessment being conducted? Are they in the moment during a lesson, a planned-for interaction decided before the class, or a curriculum embedded to gather data at a significant point in the learning process (Fleischer et al. 2013)?
3. What type of assessment is it? Is it a teacher observation, a conversation with a student or group of students, or an artifact of learning?

Armed with what to look for, as an observer, each time you see formative assessment happening, use the table to write the following:

- Who is formatively assessing in the first column
- How they are being assessed in the second column
- The type of assessment occurring in the third column
- The specifics of the formative assessment activity in the last column

Combined, all of this information will arm both the teacher and the observer, especially over time, with all the information needed to examine formative assessment usage and, if desired, suggestions for growth (see table 7.4).

Final Thoughts

- A graded quiz is not a formative assessment.
- Quick, "do students get it" mass formative assessments like thumbs up/down, red-yellow-green, and fist-to-five have limited value as formative assessments because it is difficult to know if students are being honest. It

is therefore recommended that their use be limited and used only for simple concepts.

- "One characteristic that separates good teaching from masterful teaching is the teacher's routine use of formative assessment techniques that are embedded in every lesson" (Venables and Venables, as cited in Ferlazzo 2014).

Table 7.4. Formative Assessment and Knowing What Each Student Has Learned to Guide Next Steps

Who: Teacher; Peer-to-Peer with; Student;	How: In the Moment; Planned for; Embedded	Type: Observations; Conversations; Artifacts of Learning	Assessment Specifics

Toolbox Possibilities: Interviews; Conferring; 10-2/Chunk 'n' Chew; Cooperative Learning; Questioning; Note Taking; Graphic Organizers; Exit Slips; Rubrics; Exemplars; Demonstration Station; Examples/Non-examples; Mini-Whiteboards; 10-, 50-, 100-Word Summary; 3 Things; Analogy; Metacognition Exit; Back Channel; Draw It; 1 Minute; Online Quiz; Plickers; Photo Capture; New Clothes; Do's & Don'ts; Yes/No chart; Explain What Matters; Venn Diagram; Non-graded Quizzes; Self and Peer Assessment

DESCRIPTIVE PROGRESS FEEDBACK

Rationale

Once students have been assessed formatively, one of the immediate next steps is using that information to guide students on the path toward understanding and transference of the learning (Intel 2007). Feedback comes into play when teachers adopt a working assumption that effective feedback provides specific suggestions for closing the gap between where students are and where they need to be in relation to the learning goal (Moss and Brookhart 2009).

Evidence clearly points to the effectiveness of the use of feedback. As Grant Wiggins (2012) points out, "Decades of education research support the idea that by teaching *less* and providing *more* feedback, we can produce greater learning." Feedback is most effective when characterized as follows:

- It is nonevaluative, specific and personalized, actionable, timely, ongoing, and related to the learning goals and provides opportunities for the student to revise and improve work products and deepen understandings while there is still time to act on it (Chappuis 2012; Fleischer et al. 2013; Wiggins 2012).
- It points out strengths in the work and gives guidance for improvement (Chappuis 2012).
- Teachers find that "just right" line between giving too much information and not enough (Chappuis 2012).
- It avoids comparing students, creating competition among students, or referencing student ability in any way that limits motivation (Black and Wiliam 1998).

When the feedback is done well, learners will be able to answer these questions:

- Am I on the right track?
- What improvements can I make?
- What am I doing well?
- How am I doing overall? (Chappuis 2012)

With effective feedback, a learner will be able to successfully self-monitor and have higher aspirations for further achievement, greater self-satisfaction, and higher performance overall (Intel 2007).

Completing This Section

Before moving forward, it is important to share more detailed information on two elements of feedback: who is giving it and the type given.

Who? There are three different categories of people who give feedback—teachers, peers, and self—and they give it in four different ways:

Provide Informal Teacher Feedback. This gives learners on-the-spot responses to work in which they are immersed at the time in order to make sure they are on the right track. Informal feedback is a vitally important element in providing effective feedback. Teachers answer questions, provide suggestions, or just check in with learners to see how they are progressing. It is done to quickly steer students in the right direction or to enhance learning. It is most regularly one or more of the following:

- Periodic checkup
- Stop by a learner's desk
- Written response in a learning log or on the work itself (Intel 2007; New South Wales Department of Education 2015)

Provide Formal Teacher Feedback. This is given through structured conferences with specific goals. Dialogue focuses on suggestions and comments along with individualized goal setting on a formal level. Helpful hints include the following:

- Looking at learner work beforehand
- A feedback form accompanying the work that learners can take with them
- Focus on two to three items that need work and being prepared to share examples on how to improve them
- Sharing plenty of positive feedback
- Time for the learner to ask questions and give input (Intel 2007)

Provide Peer-to-Peer Feedback. Students, by looking at the work of a peer, find themselves automatically thinking about and evaluating their own work for areas of success and improvement that deepens their own understanding of their work in relation to the target (New South Wales Department of Education 2015). Keys to success include the following:

- Training students how to do it
- Providing learners with a peer feedback form
- Providing students with criterion-based rubrics to help guide students in knowing what to look for when assessing peers' work (Intel 2007)

Provide Self-Feedback. This is when students review their own work, usually against a rubric or exemplar, and then make notes and/or changes to their work based on their comparison. Self-feedback always follows self-formative assessment.

Types of Feedback

Three main types of feedback are given: basic, instructional, and coaching:

1. **Basic** feedback tells students if they were right or wrong while also providing the correct answer. Research shows that the simple act of providing the correct answer has far more impact than telling them just the result. Basic feedback works best with students who have some mastery of the material; therefore, basic feedback is best used with advanced and intermediate learners. Basic feedback works best when you ask the students to prove that the answer you gave them is correct (Killian 2017).
2. **Instructional** feedback is when teachers provide suggestions to students on how their work can be improved or fixed. Teachers offer concrete and specific information about next steps. Instructional feed-

back works really well with struggling and novice learners. This feedback could involve reteaching an entire concept or process but usually provides specific details on what to do differently next time. Instructional feedback usually concludes with teachers giving a worked example to follow and a practice problem that the teacher and student work out together (Killian 2017).

3. **Coaching** feedback is the art of using hints and prompts to help students help themselves. Coaching feedback is about developing self-efficacy. This underused strategy is best used with students who are proficient in the area they are studying because the guidance is vague. Often, coaching feedback follows instructional feedback as students become more proficient (Killian 2017).

Now, armed with what to look for, as an observer, each time you see descriptive progress feedback happening, use the table to write who is giving the feedback: teacher informal, teacher formal, peer-to-peer, or self in the first column. In the second column, write the type of feedback: basic, instructional, or coaching. In the last column, add relevant specific feedback details. Specific quotes given by the teacher can be especially useful in the reflective conversation. Over time, a picture of a teacher's use of feedback will emerge (see table 7.5).

Final Thoughts

- There is a powerful connection between feedback and collaborative learning; experience has shown that cooperative learning structures function as

Table 7.5. Descriptive Progress Feedback

Who: Teacher informal; Teacher formal; Peer-to-peer; Self	Type: Basic Instructional Coaching	Feedback Specifics

Toolbox Possibilities: Modeling; Peer Coaching; Self-Coaching; Rubrics; Exemplars; Conferring; Met, Not Yet Met, I Noticed; More of, Less of; What's Working? What's Not? What's Next? Highlighters; Traffic Lights; Post-It Notes; Two Stars and a Wish; Margins; But What if You Did?

a highly effective peer-to-peer feedback tool. When students use cooperative learning structures, they give and receive feedback following each problem they solve, and, important to their success, they receive the feedback immediately rather than having it delayed until after the teacher has had time to grade their worksheets. This change allows students to improve as they practice rather than getting feedback following potentially bad practice. Frequency and immediacy of feedback are increased tremendously (Kagan 2014).

- Not surprisingly, the effect of feedback done well is the same for teacher–student relationships and observer–teacher relationships. In both instances, trusting, supportive relationships are key to growth. Jan Chappuis (2012), formative assessment expert, writes, "Regardless of what treatment is in her best interest, she only wants to take the advice of the ones she trusts. . . . By looking closely at their work to understand what they understand and identify where they need help, we are listening to our students. Our feedback can communicate to them that we have heard them, and they will be more likely to trust us enough to follow our advice for that sometimes-difficult next step." Feedback works only when students trust teachers, just like feedback works only when teachers trust principals.

SPECIFIC DIFFERENTIATION

Rationale

> More than a century ago . . . the teacher in a one-room schoolhouse faced a challenging task. She had to divide her time and energy between teaching young people . . . who could not read or write . . . and teaching more advanced students of varying ages who had very different content needs. Today's teachers still contend with the essential challenge of the teacher in the one-room schoolhouse: how to reach out effectively to students who span the spectrum of learning readiness, personal interests, and culturally shaped ways of seeing and speaking about and experiencing the world. —Tomlinson (2014)

Carol Ann Tomlinson, the developer of the term "differentiation" and the author of *The Differentiated Classroom*, describes this schoolhouse as a teacher's proactive response to learner needs. Teachers analyze students' needs based on assessment data and craft learning experiences that meet their needs (McCarthy 2017). Done right, this process ensures that what a student learns, how he or she learns it, and how the student demonstrates what he or she has learned is a match for that student's readiness level, interests, and preferred mode of learning (Tomlinson 2014). It is making sure that the right students get the right learning tasks at the right time. In the end, once you have a sense of what each student holds as known and what he or she needs in order to learn, differentiation is no longer an option; it is an obvious response (McCarthy 2017).

Research supports differentiation as an effective tool for enhanced learning. In one study, the average student in high school read at a 5.9 grade level. After four years of differentiated instruction, the average student read at an 8.2 grade level (Rock et al. 2008). In another study, fourteen same-grade teachers were trained in differentiated instruction for a year before the study began, and their results were compared to ten teachers who were not trained. The results showed an eleven-point gain for the differentiated students versus a one point gain for the control group in one school year.

Most encouraging of all in this study was the promise that differentiated instruction holds for equity and closing the achievement gap. Even though socioeconomic status was factored in, results showed that there was no effect of socioeconomic status on students' progress, confirming that differentiation can maximize learning outcomes for all students regardless of their socioeconomic background (Tsolaki and Koutselini 2012).

Completing This Section

Before moving forward, it is important to share more detailed information on three elements of differentiation: methods, areas, and learner voice and access.

Methods

There are two methods for differentiating instruction, namely, intuitive and intentional:

- Intuitive differentiation is the work that's done in the heat of instruction, when the lesson plans meet students (McCarthy 2017). Feedback fits into this category, as do on-the-spot adjustments to the original plans. All teachers intuitively differentiate to some degree.
- Intentional differentiation is the planning that occurs prior to instruction based on assessment data (McCarthy 2017). Teachers use formative assessment data and knowledge of students to drive this intentional planning, which can occur in areas of content, process, and/or product. Teachers also factor student readiness, interest, and learning preferences into their intentional differentiation planning.

Areas of Differentiation

There are three generally agreed-on areas where teachers can make adjustments to differentiate their instruction, namely, content, process, and product:

- Content is what students learn or need to learn or how they gain access to knowledge, understanding, or skills; the information and ideas students grapple with to reach the learning goal; how access to information is made to learners; and how learners are able to access and understand the concepts and skills.
- Process is how students learn or how the student will come to master and "own" the knowledge, ideas, and skills; how students take in and make sense of the content; and how learners digest content and make it into their own.
- Product is how students demonstrate their mastery of the knowledge or skills or how they will summatively show what they have learned; how students show what they know, understand, and can do; and how learners would distill what they learned by application, demonstration, or performance (McCarthy 2017; Tomlinson 2015).

Learner Voice and Access

There are three generally agreed-on learner voice and access areas that teachers consider when making decisions about differentiated adjustments to instruction, namely, readiness, interest, and learner preference:

- Readiness is growth, a student's proximity to specific learning goals, and what this student *needs* to do in order to succeed. Knowledge of student and formative assessment results is necessary for accurate teacher perception of readiness.
- Interests are motivation, passions, affinities, and kinships that motivate learning or a topic or skill that taps into a student's talents, experiences, or dreams. Even new possibilities that a student could encounter in the classroom that would be a source of future passions are elements of student interest.
- Learner preference consists of the preferred student approaches to learning that are most efficient and effective for them as learners. These can be shaped by gender, culture, the environment, biology, and a particular learning context (Tomlinson 2015).

Now, armed with what to look for, as an observer, each time you see evidence of differentiation happening, use the table to write the type of differentiation, intuitive or intentional, in the first column. Next, determine which area of differentiation is being targeted by the teacher—content, process, or product—and write that in the second column. For the third column, determine which area of learner voice is being accessed and tapped into by the teacher and students—readiness, interest, or learner preference—and write that down (see table 7.6).

If you are not sure which area of learner voice is being accessed, because this can sometimes be harder to gauge, do your best to write what you believe it to be. Observers don't know the students as well as the teachers and so have to make a judgment without all the information a teacher has. The important thing is noticing when learner voice is being considered and used. Finally, in the fourth column, write the details of what is being observed. As always, begin by writing the pedagogical tool and add from there.

Final Thoughts

- McCarthy's (2017) book *So All Can Learn* is highly recommended for building observer capacity and an understanding of differentiation. His work has made differentiation so much more accessible. Understanding that "in-the-moment" adjustments, descriptive feedback, and reteaching something are differentiation provides observers points of success to identify and build on with teachers.
- It is important to understand that differentiating is difficult to understand thoroughly and to put into practice effectively. It will be common to observe only in-the-moment differentiation at first, and that is okay. Use

Table 7.6. Specific Differentiation

Method: Intuitive; Intentional	Area: Content; Process; Product	Learner Voice and Access: Readiness; Interest; Learner Preference	Differentiation Specifics

Toolbox Possibilities: Flexible Grouping; Tiering; Graphic Organizers; Centers; Learning Contracts/Agendas; Small Group Instructions; Enrichment/Extensions; Think Dots/Task Cards/Think Tac Toe/Menus; Project/Problem/Performance Based Learning; RAFT; Remediation/Extension Activities; Multimedia/Technology; Conferring; Cooperative Learning; Rubrics; Chunk 'n' Chew; Learner Preference Cards; Learner Profile Quick Surveys; Compacting; Anchor Activities this evidence of in-the-moment differentiation during your reflective conversations to help develop more advanced and effective intentional differentiation.

- One of the best things about looking for and working with teachers on "evidence of differentiation" is that when observers do their jobs well, they also model differentiation well. In TBO, the model calls for observers to work with each teacher, intuitively and intentionally, on content, process, or product, and they tailor that work according to where each teacher is with his or her readiness, interest, and, often, learner preference. When observers model well, their words resonate more deeply.

- Drawing connections, when teachers formatively assess students regularly, they gain much of the information necessary to help guide differentiated instruction for each learner. Or, as McCarthy (2017) writes, "differentiation and assessments make an unbeatable combination for learner achievements." When teachers provide descriptive progress feedback tailored to a student's individual needs, they are differentiating their practice at the same time. When teachers take the time to build relationships with each of their students such that they know them as learners and by their voice, they are gaining information necessary to effectively differentiate intentionally. Further, experientially, the strongest teachers are the ones who truly know all their students as individuals.

LEARNING PRINCIPLES USED

Rationale

First, the learning principles are not an area of pedagogy to be developed, but having them on the form provides tremendous value. The pyramid provides teachers with a big-picture visual representation of the variety and frequency of the different teaching and learning activities they employ as opposed to the specific elements of observed pedagogy that are the focus of the rest of the form. There are two main goals in using the learning principles pyramid: to encourage teachers to use a wide variety of strategies that tap into all learner preferences and to increase the use of pedagogical areas that align with the bottom half of the pyramid, the areas that are more engaging and the learning more active for the students.

The famous learning pyramid (without a discussion of the percentages of learner retention rates for teaching and learning activities) is the basis of this section. The tidy original five- and ten-point increments of the percentages for each level of the pyramid have been debunked, and people realize that the ability of a single strategy to be singularly effective without taking into consideration learners doesn't make sense. However, there is definitely agreement among educators that the logic behind the percentages holds true.

The strategies at the bottom of the pyramid generally are more effective at creating a greater depth of learning than those at the top. The truth is that almost all teachers use multiple pedagogical strategies each day in their teaching to impact learning. There is no doubt that combinations of strategies are going to improve learning more than using one or two pedagogical teaching strategies. For example, if a teacher primarily lectures, then the learning impact will be limited. If, however, a teacher uses collaborative learning and working memory pedagogical strategies in conjunction with lecture, then the retention of learning will be much higher because collaborative learning and working memory strategies involve the higher-retention learning principles of discussion and teaching others.

When teachers see the visual evidence of the variety of strategies they use not only over the course of an individual lesson but, even more important, also cumulatively for evidence of a pattern over multiple class observations, it is good food for thought.

Completing This Section

As an observer, one of the first things to do when beginning an observation is to write down the current teaching or learning activity in the learning pyramid table. Determine the type of activity and write it in the proper row using words from the "Toolbox Possibilities." Next, use the "Frequency" column to keep a tally by making a mark in the appropriate box. Repeat this process each time a different activity occurs. For this section, because the observer is often writing about the activity in a different section as well, there is no need to provide detail beyond naming it.

An additional point regarding learning principles is that, as an observer, sometimes it can be difficult to pinpoint exactly where an activity fits on the pyramid. An activity might not feel like it aligns directly with any of the

LEARNING PRINCIPLES USED:

	FREQUENCY	LEARNING PRINCIPLE ACTIVITY SPECIFICS
LECTURE		
READING		
AUDIO VISUAL		
DEMONSTRATION		
DISCUSSION GROUP		
PRACTICE BY DOING		
TEACHING OTHERS		

learning principles. In those instances, do your best to put it in the column that is subjectively judged to be the best fit.

Final Thoughts

• Although learning principles do not concern a single specific instructional strategy, the use of this pyramid has proven valuable time and again. By taking the time to quickly jot down each activity in the line that most accurately reflects it, a clear visual representation of the variety of strategies employed by teachers is shown. When teachers see their tendency to stay on the top of the pyramid, they notice and often make changes on their own just by looking at the table.

• The use of a variety of strategies is appropriate and to be encouraged. There are times when direct instruction must include lecture or reading or some audiovisual method. Share this information with teachers who might get defensive. Certainly, however, adding in working memory activities will help learning.

• Without exception, teachers have appreciated the visual representation of the variety and frequency of strategies they use.

STUDENT INTERVIEW (IS LEARNING CLEAR TO ALL?)

Can students articulate what their LT is and why it has value (as an extension or for further use in life)? Can students demonstrate the learning of their target—how they know they have learned it?

Rationale

In many ways, the student interview is the most important element of the observation. The observation and the form are incomplete without the interview. The observation's effectiveness as a tool to improve teaching and learning is limited without knowing the answers to the questions. That's because students' answers to these questions help determine if learning aligns with teaching.

The seemingly best teaching in the world means very little if students can't explain what they are learning and why it has meaning. If students can't regularly identify their learning, describe it, demonstrate it, and show its relevance, then there is a problem. Student interview answers serve as de facto checks and balances for learning. Observers ask these questions to ensure that teaching and learning align.

Without asking these questions, mostly what is known is what was taught. There is some sense of what is learned from observing teachers formatively assess, give feedback, and intuitively differentiate their instruction, but full knowledge of what was learned is limited. Together, observation and student interviews provide a more complete picture of learning. Asking these questions helps gauge teaching effectiveness.

Not interviewing students about their learning and just assuming that the students have learned the targets is much like a teacher holding a traditional question-and-answer session where they ask questions, repeatedly call on the few students who raise their hands, and then assume that all the students get it. A handful of students answering questions correctly doesn't mean that all students get it, just like it doesn't mean that students are learning just because all the boxes on the LT table are checked. Neither teachers nor observers can afford to assume otherwise.

Completing This Section

As an observer, it is easy to find reasons not to do the student interview. Observers sometimes feel that the type of activity going on is one that is best left undisturbed by an interview. Sometimes, observers feel like, with only twenty minutes, time is better spent solely observing teaching. No matter the reason, *find the time*—the student answers serve as too valuable a tool to not be done each and every observation.

Because of the variability of kids and their developmental levels and backgrounds, explaining how to successfully complete this section is a little more involved than the rest of the form. First, interview multiple students. Although observers don't have time to ask questions of each student during a twenty-minute observation, there is time to ask the questions to more than one student. More answers equals more information. Asking more than one student is especially important when the first student asked can't give evidence of the connection between learning and teaching.

As an observer, it becomes quickly apparent which students get things more easily, which students get things somewhere in the middle of the pack, and which students tend to struggle to get things. Strive to ask students of perceived varying levels of readiness in order to gain a more well-rounded picture of student understanding.

It is common to find that it is difficult for students to answer or know how to answer the questions, especially when beginning TBO and students aren't used to being interviewed or of having observers in the classroom frequently. Also, realize that, depending on where your school is in its development, some teachers will be less experienced with LTs. Because there can be significant variance on the effectiveness of teacher use of LTs, there will be accompanying variance on student understanding of the questions being asked, especially at first.

Depending on the age of the students and their experience with hearing these questions, guidance is necessary. It's okay to help students answer the questions, especially at first and with younger students. If they aren't sure what you are asking, point them to the LT in the room and then ask again. It can also be effective to model the answer so that next time they will have a better understanding of what you are looking for from them.

Over time, students do begin to expect the questions and gain a better sense of how to answer. As students expect to answer questions about learning, not coincidentally, teachers improve their usage and formative assessments of LTs. As a result, students are able to more effectively answer the questions. Of course, some students will regularly require a little observer guidance on how to answer the questions. Through guidance and patience, observers will find that more and more students are able to answer the questions.

The bottom line is, as an observer, to ask the questions, help students when needed, and write their answers. Whatever students can or cannot answer is okay. At worst, there are opportunities for growth.

Final Thoughts

- Again, the student interview questions make the form complete. The answers to these questions are powerful indicators of effectiveness; they show observers and teachers the alignment between teaching and learning.
- When students can regularly answer the questions with specifics that indicate understanding of the learning, this information helps observers to gain pictures of what strong teacher effectiveness looks like. Knowing the teachers who are particularly strong at aligning teaching and learning provides observers with a list of potential teacher leaders who can lead professional development.
- When students can't answer the questions in ways that ensure observers that teaching and learning align, observers know that the obvious place to begin growth conversations will center on the different elements of LTs.
- When the answers are somewhere in the middle, observers know that growth conversations will probably center on specific differentiation practices.

ON TEACHING INTANGIBLES, SCRIPTING, ADDITIONAL PEDAGOGY, QUESTIONS, AND SUGGESTIONS

This section of the form allows observers to write about areas unaddressed in the rest of the form. In this section, observers can write the following:

- Teaching intangibles
- Specific quotes that teachers and/or students use that have value for later
- Effective teaching strategies witnessed that the form doesn't address
- Questions that arise over the course of an observation
- Suggestions, either to be addressed immediately or to be saved for another time

TEACHING INTANGIBLES

Rationale

Good teaching cannot be reduced to technique. People who do good work of any sort understand that not everything they need to know can be found in data points and cognitive constructs. Good teachers and leaders bring at least as much art as science to their work (Palmer 2017). If teaching is an art that "calls for intuition, creativity, and improvisation," surely we should be celebrating, awarding, and encouraging unique, personalized, diverse teaching practices? We should, but we don't! Instead, we have a system that is attempting, through lesson observation, to pigeonhole teaching practices by formula and rules to create uniformed "good teachers" and "good teaching practices" (O'Leary 2017).

Having teaching intangibles on the form allows observers to expand beyond the limits of the observation form and beyond concrete suggestions of what good teaching is. It provides a place to write about areas of teaching excellence, or "art," that aren't quantifiable in any of the other sections of the form. Success in the technical areas of teaching and the art of teaching combined create the most effective teachers. When observers honor the art and the craft of teaching, they are fostering an environment that demonstrates support for the highest form of teaching practice. In doing so, observers create an enormous safety net for teachers willing to take risks in practice.

Completing This Section

So, how do observers know when they are seeing intangibles? It's like former Supreme Court Justice Potter Stewart said: "I know it when I see it." Or, if observers know they are seeing something that's working but can't figure out where else it goes, then they have identified an intangible. As an observer, write what you notice and what strikes you. Examples of intangibles (but not all because all are not describable) include the following:

- Passion for a subject

- Teacher response to a critical moment, one in which a learning opportunity for students will open up or shut down, depending, in part, on how the teacher handles it (Palmer 2017)
- A teacher's humanness

Final Thoughts

Noticing intangibles builds trust with teachers. Good teaching "touches the soul" of those who practice it. While most discussions today focus on the technical dimensions of teaching and its enhancement, that teachers' humanness is very much a part of their practice is important to remember, and teachers need expressions of personal regard and support as much as anyone else does (Bryk and Schneider 2002). Further, building relationship in honoring their "art" is an important element of having teachers embrace creativity and risk taking. When observers embrace the art of teaching, they begin to support what might be seen by some as unusual or unorthodox methods of excellence. This is the first step: to accommodate the wide differences and needs of the very able (Greenleaf 2002).

SCRIPTING

Rationale

As previously discussed when writing about the origins of TBO, there is great value in teachers seeing their own words written down. Having it still on the form allows observers to capture moments or words worthy of discussion later.

Completing This Section

Write the words that strike you.

ADDITIONAL PEDAGOGY

Rationale

In limiting the number of elements of good teaching practice that the form looks for, there are many pedagogical strategies that are effective but aren't listed. Having additional pedagogy on the form allows observers to have a place to write about these areas.

Completing This Section

Name the strategy and write any details you wish to share.

QUESTIONS

Rationale

Although there are questions that are asked during the reflective conversations, it is inevitable that on occasion other questions will arise during some observations. Having questions here provides observers with a place to write those questions. Writing questions in the body of the form runs the risk of distracting the teacher from the noticed strengths. By writing them here, that issue is eliminated.

Completing This Section

Write any questions that arise here. Leave them here if they will be addressed during the next reflective conversation. Move them to that teacher's notes document if it will be discussed later.

SUGGESTIONS

Rationale

Beginning as early as the fourth observation, observers can potentially begin to offer suggestions and support for a growth area (more on suggestions soon). This section provides a place to write suggestions that doesn't interfere with teachers embracing the sharing of strengths in the reflective conversation. Quick fixes can be addressed here as well. For example, a minor suggestion, such as making sure the LT is not just on a PowerPoint but also displayed on the whiteboard so that it can be seen by the entire class, could be written here.

Completing This Section

Write suggestions here. Feel free to write them during any visit. If they are not going to be suggested at the next visit, then move them to that teacher's notes document.

Chapter Eight

Questions

No uniform set of questions will apply with equal force to the many varieties in which good teaching comes. —Parker Palmer

Questions are first discussed here because they are listed on the observation form. As an observer, you have the freedom to ask any questions that might arise during the course of an observation or reflective conversation. These questions may be about the methods of good teaching witnessed, a concern, uncertainty, or anything else that sparks curiosity. Although you are free to ask anything, having a uniform set of initial reflective questions turns out to be an excellent starting point on the road to growth. The value of these questions, listed on the form, is the focus of this chapter. Later, the questions will be visited again from the perspective of the reflective conversation. The first two questions are the following:

1. What were you doing to help students learn?
2. If you had it to do over again, what, if anything, would you do differently?

These seemingly simple questions have stood the test of time. They are nonthreatening, and they put teachers in the proper mindset to think about and reflect on their teaching choices and how those actions affect student learning. These questions have proven impactful in at least three different ways:

1. They build safe and trusting relationships with teachers, which is key to maximizing improved teaching and learning because when teachers feel safe, they are more willing to take risks in their practice. These questions, from the beginning, have proven to feel nonthreatening to teachers. In fact, teachers are surprised and excited that you are even asking for their opinions, as if wanting to know what they thought was foreign to them.

What they enjoy most about being asked the questions is the simple sense that they are being treated like respected professionals whose thoughts are valued. They appreciate that someone is curious about their process and is listening to them. This description might sound silly, but over and over again, teachers have said that this is the first time they have ever been asked what *they* thought.

So, the use of these questions, which demonstrates a genuine interest in hearing what a teacher has to say about their teaching, is the beginning of the building of trusting relationships between observer and observee. Teachers immediately feel more valued because their opinions are valued and they are being listened to by their principals. Just the process of asking and listening nonjudgmentally builds trust.

2. The answers to these questions give administrators much insight into teachers. You learn about their vision, their understanding of teaching and learning, and the connection between the two. You gain insight into their self-awareness, their planning process, their reflective process, their mind-sets, and their feelings about students—high-achieving students, average students, low-achieving students, difficult students, and students overall. Their answers provide much information that can be used to make decisions on how to best work with, guide, and support their growth.

3. These questions send a message, in a positive, constructive way, that self-reflection and dialogue about teaching and learning are expected, regular, and valued elements of the teaching process. This comment is made with the full realization that many teachers are already incredibly self-reflective, constantly reviewing each lesson in their heads and deciding on what went well and what went poorly in order to guide the next steps.

Before moving on, it feels important to share that teachers' overwhelmingly positive reactions to these simple inquiry questions shine an unflattering light on teacher perceptions of the traditional observation process. These teacher responses indicate that the absence of a feeling of partnership has been the norm for most teachers during the observation process, a process that is still largely evaluatively graded, infrequent, and formal and more about telling teachers what to fix and not about asking and listening to teachers share their thoughts and reasoning for their choices.

These experiences, which engender negative feelings for teachers about the evaluation process, are an obstacle to growth. The hope is that the use of these questions, combined with observers tapping into their emotional intelligence and empathy during reflective conversations, will rid teachers of these negative feelings about observations and instead lead to increased risk taking and improved learning. Other questions on the TBO form are the following:

- Question of the year
- What progress have you made on your action research big goal?
- Is there anything specific you would like me to look for on the next visit or anything you would like me to add about this visit?

Question of the year: Each school seems to have common areas of growth for most teachers. The areas might be different at each school, but there are usually a couple of areas of pedagogy where a schoolwide professional development focus on them would help almost all teachers. It has always made sense to spend an entire year focused on schoolwide professional development in the target area.

If in the observation process a question could be added that is tied to this area, it would help keep that area of pedagogical growth even more in the forefront of everyone's mind. After all, teachers are not only working on it all year but also regularly being asked about their progress with that pedagogical area. Thus was born the question of the year, a yearly schoolwide question connected to an annual professional development growth area.

Now an entire school year is spent aligning focused professional development activities with a pedagogical goal; through the reflective conversation, teachers are asked a related question to check in regularly on their progress. Having a yearly point of pedagogical focus backed by a question has proven to be energizing and supportive of enormous schoolwide growth. Teachers actually like the accountability that being asked the question adds.

As an example of a question of the year, one school had room for substantial improvement with formative assessment. So a question of the year was created, really a miniseries of questions: "What did you do to formatively assess whether 'each' student attained sufficient progress toward their LT? Based on the results of these assessments, meaning either most got it, some got it, or not many got it, what adjustments, if any, might you make to your plans?" Teachers were asked these questions, tied to their professional development at every reflective conversation.

After working as a principal for some time, it became apparent that, for many, yearly goals tended to be created and worked on at the beginning of the year and then forgotten, or at least not regularly and actively focused on during the course of the year, that is, until May, when the e-mail reminder from the principal about "end-of-year evaluation and goal reflection" is sent out. Many would then frantically search for their goal document, hoping they had made progress. The goals were in their heads on some level; they were often worked on in some manner, but the big panic came at the end of the year when it was time to detail their success in achieving the goals.

So the action research big goal question was added, much like the question of the year, to keep those goals regularly present in the teacher thought process. If teachers know they are going to be asked about their goals regularly during the reflective conversation, then chances are much higher that they will stay present in teachers' minds and are actively worked on regularly. For teachers who struggle with staying on top of their goals (and even those who don't), periodic accountability checks help. Many teachers report that they appreciate the accountability because it forces them to work on their goals regularly. Many teachers also appreciate the chance to regularly talk about and get feedback on their progress with their goals. For those wondering what action research big goals are, details will be explained in chapter 19.

Is there anything specific you would like me to look for on the next visit? Is there anything else you would like me to add to the form? It was important to do everything possible to make sure teachers knew that this process is about and for them. So it made sense to end the reflective conversation with a final check-in. The result is these questions. They are different than the other questions in that they are asked at the end of the conversation, not the beginning.

In practice, teachers don't often ask for something to be looked for on the next visit or to have something added to the observation form. The questions do accomplish what was intended: sending a message that a teacher's thoughts and feelings are valued.

FINAL THOUGHTS

- Although these are the questions that are asked after every observation, this doesn't preclude the observer from asking anything else that comes to mind.
- Some people wonder if asking this many questions during the course of a reflective conversation will take too long. First, all these questions work to maximize teacher growth and student learning while building trusting relationships with teachers, so how can they not be asked? Second, experience has shown that reflective conversations, even when discussing these questions, normally take only between ten and twenty minutes. The question to ask is, where is your time worth the most? When the answer is, where it will have the greatest impact on student learning, then this time is well spent.

Chapter Nine

Web Links

Trust-Based Observations as a Resource Tool

One of the unique elements of the TBO form is its dual functionality. It serves not only as an observation form to identify strengths and growth opportunities but also as a resource form. Under each "Evidence of" heading, you see the words "Toolbox Possibilities," followed by a list of pedagogical strategies representative of potential good teaching ideas fitting into that category: Formative Assessment/Knowing What Each Student Has Learned to Guide Next Steps (Toolbox Possibilities): Interviews; Conferring; 10-2/ Chunk 'n' Chew; Cooperative Learning; Questioning; Note Taking; Graphic Organizers; Exit Slips; Rubrics; Exemplars; Demonstration Station; Examples/Non-examples; Mini-Whiteboards; 10-, 50-, 100-Word Summary; 3 Things; Analogy; Metacognition Exit; Back Channel; Draw It; 1 Minute; Online Quiz; Plickers; Photo Capture; New Clothes; Do's & Don'ts; Yes/No chart; Explain What Matters; Venn Diagram; Non-graded Quizzes; Self and Peer Assessment)

These lists of strategies serve a dual purpose. They serve as reminders to observers of what some of the strategies in these areas are. Having them written down on the form aids observers in looking for or noticing what is going on in the classroom. These lists of strategies allow observers to use very specific language when documenting evidence of good practice.

More uniquely, they serve as a learning resource tool for teachers. In the electronic version of the form, readers can click on any of the "Toolbox Possibilities," and they are sent to a Web page full of resources for that area of pedagogy. It provides recommendations on the best books for learning more about that strategy. It also provides numerous Web links to articles with learning opportunities pertaining to each strategy.

For example, when you click on "Toolbox Possibilities" in the "Working Memory" section, the new Web page that pops up will offer not only book recommendations but also links to general articles about the use of working memory. Next, readers will also see Web links to numerous articles with instructions or practical tips on how to improve or adopt any of the activities listed on the form.

Teachers and observers alike can use these learning resources to add to and enhance practice. In the reflective conversations, teachers and observers can use these links to engage in more productive conversations on ways to grow. They just pull up a Web link to a new strategy right there during their discussion.

As a note, the "Toolbox Possibilities" lists are abridged, and the lists of Web links are a continual work in progress. E-mail suggestions to craig@trustbased.com so that additional tools and references can be added. Feel free to send Web links for articles, too.

Part 4

The Reflective Conversation

Chapter Ten

Reflective Conversation System Basics

Ultimately, TBO leads here, to the reflective conversation. These meetings are where everything comes together; it's where trust, the foundation for risk taking, is most developed. In adopting TBO's reflective conversation system, you will see teachers make enormous changes.

For starters, as you know, the system prescribes three reflective conversations per day, Tuesday through Friday. So, what do these follow-up chats look like?

Yesterday's observations are completed, and now on most days, in addition to the next three observations, there are three reflective conversations to have with teachers. Not surprisingly, being well prepared for these conversations is essential for making each one as successful as possible. Knowing the organizational steps and fundamentals of the system is also imperative to fostering growth. This chapter guides observers through these basic priorities.

PRIORITIZE REFLECTIVE CONVERSATIONS

First, it's important to prioritize the reflective conversations, even over the observations. Remember, depending on the school and its method of scheduling, teachers can normally have anywhere from one to three preparation/ planning periods per day. So, because the window for reflective conversations is smaller than the window for observations, look at the schedules of all the teachers you plan to visit each day to make sure you are creating your proposed daily schedule in a way that prioritizes doing the reflective conversations first.

During class periods when teachers due for a reflective conversation have a prep period and teachers to be observed teach, all else being equal, do the reflective conversation first. Doing so is crucial to getting in all the conversations every day. Also, depending on the length of classes, often both the conversation and the observation can be completed in the same period.

What about when an observer misses the teacher for the reflective conversation? The reality is that you can have a schedule of observations and conversations ready for the day but the conversations don't work out according to plan. Usually, it's the unpredictable nature of the job: emergencies come up, or a teacher isn't in the room during a prep period. When a teacher isn't in the room, a brief immediate e-mail to the teacher saying that you missed her and checking if time is available that period often leads to a meeting later that day. If that doesn't work and you aren't able to get the conversation in at any other time during the day, the first priority is to find that teacher right after the school day ends and have the reflective conversation then.

On days when meeting teachers after school doesn't work either, e-mail them to schedule the conversation for before school, during their prep period, or after school the next day. Asking teachers what time works best for them has proven to be the most effective way to get the reflective conversation done. As discussed earlier, memories fade quickly, so absolutely get the conversation in this second day.

ORGANIZATION

Knowing that organization helps fuel success, what are the preparation elements necessary for reflective conversation success? First, make sure the appropriate documents are open on your laptop. The documents to include are the following:

- *Observation tracking spreadsheet* to ensure that the conversations are marked when completed.
- *TBO/reflection form* for each teacher you visited yesterday. Having the form is respectful of the teacher's valuable time, a respect that builds trust.
- *Action research big goal documents* for reflective conversation teachers. Having these documents open when asking about their big goal progress provides for greater accountability and depth of conversation on the goal. Reading and sharing knowledge of their goal demonstrates caring, which also builds trust.

It's important to quickly review what was written the day before in order to best game-plan for the reflective conversation. This review reminds observers what to highlight with teachers. It also provides an opportunity to make sure that everything written is something that you want shared with teachers during the conversation. If there are things to share later, perhaps a secondary suggestion, or a note on something to keep an eye on during the next visit, shift those to that teacher's notes document. Minimize anything that interferes with trust building.

If this visit is one where suggestions will be offered, more than a quick review is necessary. Details on that preparation are shared in chapter 14.

RESPECT

Have the Conversation in the Teacher's Classroom

The daily schedule is ready, documents are open, and the previous day's observation forms have been reviewed; now it's time for the actual reflective conversation. Go find the teacher in his room. It's so much better to have the conversation there: it's the teacher's turf, curriculum materials and examples of student work are there, and being at the "scene of the crime" is a good memory prompt for busy administrators (Marshall 2013). The most important reason, though, is to build trust.

Teachers feel more comfortable in their own space. No matter how you might try to couch it, having the conversation in the principal's office, just like for students, feels like being "called into the principal's office." This feeling will inevitably interfere with creating and maintaining a safe and trusting relationship. Teachers feel safer in their own space, and principals demonstrate respect by having the conversation in the teacher's room.

Ask Permission

When you first enter the room, now that you have done all of your preparation, it is important to ask permission to have the reflective conversation. There are times when teachers might be in the middle of something they have to get done before the next class, so extending this courtesy demonstrates respect for them and their time, a courtesy that builds relationship. Rare is the time when teachers don't engage in the conversation right then.

Sit beside the Teacher

Sitting across from the teacher provides a negative effect similar to meeting in the principal's office. To alleviate the potentially confrontational feeling that sitting across from someone can convey and, even more, to build a sense that the process is collaborative, sit beside the teacher. This also conveys transparency. A "view" version of the observation/reflection document is always shared with teachers at the end of the conversation, but when sitting beside them, teachers can see everything typed as it's being typed. This level of transparency adds a layer of comfort to the conversation that builds trust.

It's not always easy to find the best way to sit beside the teacher for the conversation. Here is some guidance. If the teacher is at her desk, the easiest thing to do is pull up a student desk beside her so she can easily see your laptop screen. The same goes if she is sitting somewhere else in the room. If she is standing somewhere, ask her where she'd like to sit. As a courtesy, ask if she'd mind if you sat beside her. The author has not been turned down yet.

THE CONVERSATION

Transcribing Teacher Answers to Questions

You're seated, and the document is open; begin by asking, "What were you doing to help students learn?" The details of what to write and how to reframe teacher words into pedagogical terms that more accurately answer the questions are explained in chapter 12. The important thing is to convey teacher answers as accurately as possible, especially because teachers are often looking at what you type. Observers usually find that as they are writing, the act of working hard to accurately portray teacher meaning helps in being a better and more engaged active listener.

As teachers finish answering each question and you finish typing, read back what you have written. Making sure you have accurately conveyed their meaning provides the added bonus of demonstrating care for accuracy, which builds relationship.

Sharing "Evidence Of"

Now that you have asked the questions, it's time to share evidence of strengths you noticed during the observation. The details on sharing "Evidence of" will be explained in chapter 13. The only reminder offered here is to make sure that any suggestions that might imply judgment be moved to the bottom of the form ahead of the conversation.

Offering Suggestions

Suggestions are offered judiciously, especially when one is new to using TBO. The next step, though, is offering suggestions when you are ready and you feel the teacher is ready for growth. The details of how to offer suggestions are explained in chapter 14.

Professional Development

Often, concurrent with offering suggestions are professional development opportunities. The details of blending professional development with the reflective conversation and TBO areas of pedagogy will be explained in detail in chapter 19. For now, suffice it to say that professional development connects to individual growth opportunities for teachers through myriad methods.

Sharing the Form and Marking the Conversation Finished

The conversation finishes by ensuring that teachers are okay with everything written on the form. You ask the last of the questions now and make any last notes. Next, you share the form with the teacher right then, making sure to send him a "View" only copy. The very last thing to do before you leave is to go to the observation tracking spreadsheet and highlight that teacher's observation yellow to indicate that the reflective conversation is completed.

Specials

Twice a year, once per semester, you will include this extra element in the reflective conversation. Teachers will have the opportunity to show you the connection between their learning targets from the lesson observed, goals from their current unit plans, and summative assessments for that unit. The details of checking for this alignment will be explored in chapter 15.

Chapter Eleven

Building Trusting Relationships

Legitimacy begins with trust. No matter what the competence or the intentions, if trust is lacking, nothing happens.—Robert Greenleaf

Actions that school leaders take every day have the potential to build or erode trust. Every conversation or e-mail with a teacher, parent, or student has the power to influence relationships, as does every faculty meeting or staff bulletin. Like it or not, principals will be judged on these contacts, which will influence perceptions of you. These contacts and actions have the power to strengthen or to bruise the development of trusting relationships. Be deliberate in these interactions because it matters. The design of TBO reflective conversations helps build trust:

- The continuous cycle of frequent visits allows observers to spend significant, regular blocks of time, foundational for relationships, engaging in reflective talks.
- Having the conversations sitting beside teachers, in their room, builds trust. Power barriers are minimized by meeting in their space and not sitting across from them.
- Beginning the conversations by asking questions provides observers with the opportunity to listen first, a crucial component in learning about teachers and building relationships.
- The positive nature of noticing "Evidence of" strengths builds relationship because teachers appreciate and feel more comfortable with leaders who share observed strengths.
- By your focusing only on strengths and not offering suggestions, the first three visits build trust as teachers realize you're not out to get them.
- Being purposeful about when and how to offer suggestions demonstrates care and understanding of each teacher and therefore builds relationships.

The reflective conversations format supports the building of trusting relation-ships, but there are even more important factors and actions that work to build trust with teachers. Chief among these is developing an understanding of what it's like for teachers to be observed and using that understanding to guide observer actions that support and spark teacher willingness to take risks. When observers understand the feelings of vulnerability that teachers experience when being observed, they have greater empathy for them. When observers also empathize with the other challenges of teaching and use their emotional intelligence during their interactions with teachers, it leads to more compassionate action in the reflective conversations.

TBO's reflective conversation design, combined with these understand-ings and subsequent observer actions, is the foundation that builds safe and trusting relationships with teachers. The power of using these tools to build trust cannot be overstated. Offering suggestions and providing support and instructional coaching are significantly more likely to result in teaching growth when teachers trust their boss. Teachers grow when they trust, when they feel safe and supported, especially during these inherently vulnerable conferences. They feel empowered, and they embrace suggestions, resulting in risk taking and innovative new practice.

This chapter helps observers develop trusting relationships with teachers by exploring vulnerability, empathy, and emotional intelligence as well as actions that build or inhibit trust.

VULNERABILITY

To shed light on the vulnerability that a teacher who is being observed feels, imagine a couple of hypothetical workplace observation scenarios. Imagine working as a barista at a coffee shop and having your boss sit down at a table, pull out her laptop, and take notes while watching you do your job for the next twenty to eighty minutes. She doesn't say anything when she's done; she just gets up and leaves, smiling or acknowledging you in some way if you're lucky. You have no sense of how things went; you just have to wait.

The next day (more likely a few days later), if you're lucky, your boss invites you into a meeting in her office and sitting behind her desk tells you what she saw. She proceeds to share her developmental ("evaluative") rat-ings of a seemingly inordinately large number of different barista skill areas. These ratings are on a scale of 1 to 4, ranging from "needs improvement" to "outstanding." She offers advice on what to get better at. It might be one area with suggestions on how to improve; it might be a number of areas without any advice on how to get better. The information and ratings from this observation, which takes place on average one or two times per year, factor significantly into whether you keep your job.

How would you feel if you saw your boss walk in and plop down at the table with her laptop? Would you be calm and relaxed? Would you be scared, frightened, or nervous? Would you feel vulnerable? What if she happened to watch you on a crazy busy day? What if there were some particularly rude customers that day? What if something was wrong with the espresso machine slowing the service? How do you explain these things to the boss?

Now imagine you work in outside sales and your boss decides to meet you at your first call of the day. He takes out his laptop and sits on the side as unobtrusively as possible, telling you to act like he's not there. He watches and takes notes on the meeting. Again, this observation takes place a couple of times per year, maybe three, four, or five times if you're lucky.

The next day, he invites you into his office, tells you what he saw, and shares the long list of developmental ratings for your sales skills. You receive advice on what to do better, and maybe you're given resources on how to get there. Once again, this observation factors largely into the decision of whether to keep you. Your boss doesn't know the customers and doesn't know how long you have had a working relationship with them. How would you feel when your boss met you at the sales call?

Sounds crazy, right? No other job in the world has an observation process like that of teachers where the boss takes notes while actively watching them do their job and rates them on a large array of skills based on seeing them less than 1 percent of the time they do their job. In the best situation, a boss meets with workers the next day, but more often the boss shares the ratings days later. He might ask some questions; he might offer "developmental" advice. Too often, he will just e-mail the ratings with suggestions or "wonderings."

In any other job, the workers would probably revolt. Tell a friend who is not in education about the process of teacher evaluation. Ask her how she would feel if it were this same way in her job. She will tell you it sounds horrible.

Who would look forward to this process? Who would want to take risks in their practice knowing that it might lower their ratings? Who wouldn't feel vulnerable in this process? How comfortable and how much trust do you think you'd have in your boss with observation evaluations being conducted in this manner? Now add to this process: What's the boss like? Is the boss nice? Mean? Altruistic? A tyrant? Involved? Aloof? Transparent? Tough to read? Caring? A jerk? It all factors into how vulnerable teachers feel being observed at work doing their job.

The observation process as it currently exists is a dangerously vulnerable one for teachers. Not that vulnerability in and of itself is bad. Vulnerability is at the core of meaningful human experiences (Brown 2012). To clarify, teachers experience healthy feelings of vulnerability when taking risks on meaningful new practices that make a difference in student achievement. The problem is the *excessive* feelings of vulnerability arising from observations as they are currently done. The result is that people feel shamed, they get protective, they "armor up," they disengage (Brown 2012), and growth is extremely unlikely. As a principal who cares, who is driven to improve teaching and learning, your aim is to build trust, minimize negative observation vulnerability feelings, and replace them with feelings of support.

The bottom line is that teacher–principal trust is explained primarily by the principal's actions to develop supportive ties that relieve teachers' sense of vulnerability (Bryk and Schneider 2002). "When observers take these supportive actions, trust develops, which reduces the . . . vulnerability that teachers experience as they take on new and uncertain tasks; it facilitates teachers' efforts to innovate . . . in order to develop more effective instruction, and . . . leads to greater effort to implement successful innovations" (Hattie 2008).

When observer actions allow teachers to develop trust in the observation process, they trust their boss and feel safe and therefore are more open to experiencing the healthy vulnerability that accompanies risk-taking change efforts. "This level of trust doesn't just happen; it . . . grows over time and requires work, attention, and full engagement. Trust isn't a grand gesture—it's a growing marble collection" (Brown 2012).

EMPATHY AND EMOTIONAL INTELLIGENCE

Relational trust is built on movements of the human heart, like empathy (Palmer 2017). So, what can observers do in the reflective conversations to build trust with their teachers? Expressing empathy is a good place to start. Empathy—which is simply listening, holding space, withholding judgment, emotionally connecting, and communicating that incredibly healing message of "You're not alone"—is a strange and powerful thing (Brown 2012). This ability to understand and show that you understand another's feelings is care, which builds trust, which deepens as individuals perceive that others care about them (Bryk and Schneider 2002). When you empathize you build relational trust, which is a catalyst for innovation because it reduces the risk associated with change (Bryk and Schneider 2002).

Specifically, telling teachers that you empathize with negative vulnerability feelings associated with their previous observation experiences is a great place to begin building trust. These words send a message that you want observations to change for the better for them. Since almost all principals are former teachers whose observation experience probably mirrors their teachers' experiences, the hope is that empathizing with the challenges of teaching and observations will come easy. Besides, who wouldn't want to empathize with their teachers when, as the godfather of emotional intelligence, Daniel

Goleman (1995), author of *Emotional Intelligence: Why It Can Matter More than IQ*, adds, "The root of altruism is empathy."

Closely linked to empathy in building trusting relationships is emotional intelligence: the ability to recognize, understand, and manage your own emotions and recognize, understand, and influence the emotions of others. In practical terms, this means being aware that emotions can drive behavior and impact people (positively and negatively). It means learning how to manage those emotions, both our own and those of others, especially when under pressure (Institute for Health and Human Potential 2019).

Emotionally intelligent leaders are able to build relationships and work hard to develop the full range of emotional intelligence domains, especially self-management of emotions and empathy (Fullan 2002). The importance of using emotional intelligence and empathizing to build relationships couldn't be more clear. An unprecedented premium is placed on emotional intelligence for on-the-job success, suggesting that, at the very highest levels, competence models for leadership typically consist of anywhere from 80 to 100 percent emotional intelligence–based abilities (Goleman 1995).

Using emotional intelligence and empathy make all the difference in building trusting relationships with teachers, and the good news is that everyone can improve their empathy and emotional intelligence. So what can leaders do to build their skills in these areas? Purposeful practice during teacher interactions helps immensely. The TBO model provides significant opportunities, twelve times per week, during the reflective conversations. At each visit, observers practice sharing noticed teaching strengths; at every visit, when asking questions, they practice listening.

ACTIONS THAT BUILD TRUST

The following is an abridged list of recommended actions that observers can use to build trust. All demonstrate the effective practice of empathy or emotional intelligence:

- Practice patience and play the long game. Control the desire to immediately offer suggestions and fix things. Bite your tongue. Suspend judgment and critiques. Pause before acting, especially with the most challenging teachers.
- Understand that each teacher is a unique person; strive to read each teacher and differentiate actions and conversations based on your perceptions of each.
- Walk the talk and be of your word. Perceptions about integrity shape trust discernments. Participants expect consistency between what people say

and what they actually do. Such judgments about personal reliability are essential to trusting another (Bryk and Schneider 2002).

- Avoid using formal authority, except as a last resort. Trust increases because it is obvious that leaders have subordinated their ego and positional power. Use reasoning, persuasion, kindness, empathy, and, in short, trustworthiness instead (Greenleaf 2002). Most people have encountered the leader who hangs authority over the heads of others. In substituting these other actions, observers are using emotional intelligence to build relationships.
- When observers hear about personal issues that teachers are experiencing, expressing concern about these issues affecting lives deepens trust as individuals perceive that others are willing to extend themselves beyond what their role might formally require (Bryk and Schneider 2002).
- Hold yourself accountable for finding the potential in your teachers (Brown 2012), just like you would want teachers to do with students. Granted, with some it can be hard. The effort hopefully pays dividends with the difficult and disaffected ones and definitely pays dividends with the rest. If you treat the difficult ones the way it sometimes feels they ought to be treated, word spreads and works against your efforts.
- Demonstrate your own vulnerability in front of your teachers. Whether it's admitting a mistake or asking for help, when a leader is willing to be vulnerable with his or her subordinates, this act of vulnerability is predictably perceived as courageous by team members and inspires others to follow suit (Brown 2012).
- Let your actions be driven by your ultimate goal: improving teaching and learning. You catch more flies with honey than with vinegar, so treat your teachers with the same respect you would want your students or your own children to receive. In other words, be nice!
- Research indicates that oxytocin helps humans overcome distrust. The effect of oxytocin is specific to trusting other people and the willingness to take risks in social situations (Kosfield 2008). Being cognizant of respectful touch, when appropriate, share a thank-you or congratulatory handshake or a pat on the arm or shoulder. Use emotional intelligence to read when this action is and is not okay.

MINDSETS OR ACTIONS THAT INHIBIT TRUST

It's normal to have the actions, personalities, or mindsets of a small percentage of teachers frustrate you. It's normal when district or state pressures to achieve more faster get the best of you. When these or other forces, external or internal, get to you, tap into your improved emotional intelligence awareness instead of letting the pressure or frustrations drive your actions.

It always comes down to how you get the best out of people, and the following actions damage relationships, preventing opportunities to get the best out of teachers. As Dean Smith, the famous University of North Carolina basketball coach, said, "I learned a lot more about how to be a good coach from all the non-examples than I did from the good ones." Here are some non-examples:

- Relying on using formal authority. The position of principal comes with power, but relying on the power that accompanies the title to get things done doesn't add up to sustained meaningful growth. When strength is borrowed, weakness is built into the quality of the relationship, and authentic relationship and trust are never developed (Greenleaf 2002).
- Order or demand. People have an inherent desire to maintain their autonomy. When observers order or demand that a teacher do something, teachers pull away because they sense a threat to their freedom. Compared to gaining their cooperation or asking if you can offer a suggestion, teachers trust you less when you order them to do something. The semantic difference between ordering and suggesting can seem minimal, but the subtle differences result in enormous differences in outcomes.
- Judging, particularly quick judgments. When principals make quick assumptions for any reason about what a teacher is or isn't capable of, it manifests itself to teachers in ways they can feel. The result is that they don't trust as much and are less willing to engage in risk-taking new practice. These quick negative judgments almost become self-fulfilling prophecies for the teacher's subsequent actions.
- Playing favorites. Be cognizant of your actions and strive to treat everyone fairly. If you find yourself regularly making comparisons to the strongest teachers, then you are probably playing favorites, consciously or not. When teachers sense that principals have favorites, they talk about it with each other. Those talks often result in the nonfavored, as a group, not trusting and not risk taking.
- Impatience. Trust and relationships take time; remember that trust is built one marble at a time. It's common to want to fix things right away. Often, you will see things that can be fixed and want to make suggestions right away. When observers are impatient and fixes are offered before trust is built, before teachers feel confident that their strengths have been recognized, they tend to fear their boss. The result is often limited trust and risk taking.
- Perfectionism. Perfection isn't generally possible or sustainable, and the mindset that expects it from others works against trust building. It's not uncommon for excellent teachers to become principals and then hold teachers to the same standards to which they believe they performed. Although the mindset is understandable, the reality is that not all teachers

will be excellent and that holding them to this bar does not get the best out of them. Having perfectionistic expectations will manifest itself in ways that cause teachers to feel inadequate or resentful. The result is that they pull back and disengage, working against the goal.

- Critical mindsets often manifest as teacher bashing. When observers engage in conversations critical of teachers (a more regular occurrence than many principals would like to admit), it is likely to play out negatively in their actions. Almost everyone in a moment of extreme frustration vents about an occasional teacher action; that rare moment of blowing off steam is not the critical mindset being described here. Principals who tend to regularly complain about teachers will find that it doesn't help in building trusting relationships. Common signs of a critical mindset include blaming, finger-pointing, and a focus on the negative. Teachers are smart and perceptive; they feel this negativity, and it inhibits trust.
- Rigid mindsets, particularly on what good teaching is. There are a nearly limitless number of ways that teachers can be excellent, many of which defy rules of best practice. When principals possess this rigid mindset on what good teaching is, the result is likely to include criticism of anything that strays from that narrow vision, resulting in teachers feeling less trustful of their supervisor.
- Shaming, belittling, and ridiculing. Whether these occur because of personal issues, mindsets, or external actions doesn't matter. What matters is using emotional intelligence to change these actions because they all work against trust building. When shame becomes a management style, engagement dies (Brown 2012).
- External pressure, not necessarily a mindset or an action but more how external pressures can interfere with an internal locus of control and therefore negatively guide actions. Examples include pressure from districts or legislators to increase scores or a desire to get ahead climbing the proverbial work ladder. These pressures have a tendency to push people to push others harder. When they worry about the outcome instead of the process of developing team members, they may survive in the short run, but they will not thrive in the long run (Gordon 2017). These actions inhibit trust. It is difficult to focus on process and building trust in these situations, but everyone will end up farther ahead when they do.

Although these mindsets, actions, and forces interfere with the development of trusting relationships, almost all principals guilty of these behaviors have the potential to change their practice and can build supportive relationships. The issues can be addressed and repaired.

Many times, these issues are best addressed through conscious self-analysis of your empathy and emotional intelligence skills. In addition, ask trusted friends, spouses, and coworkers what their opinions of your skills in these areas are. Other avenues for self-analysis and improvement include online assessments and books on improving emotional intelligence and empathy.

Principal supervisors can help, too. They can work with observers to build on or tap into observer empathy and emotional intelligence strengths. They can help by doing observations with principals and model ideal actions, working with teachers and principals from a warm, strengths-based perspective. Principal supervisors can help, assuming that they have the proper mindset, empathy, and emotional intelligence skills themselves.

Focusing on relationships isn't just a matter of boosting achievement scores for next year; it also means laying the foundation for year two and beyond. Principal efforts to motivate and energize disaffected teachers and forge relationships among otherwise disconnected teachers can have a profound effect. Well-established relationships are the resource that keeps on giving (Fullan 2002). TBO aims to use the reflective conversation to embrace the importance of trust in the drive to deliver results (Palmer 2017).

Working with teachers without developing trust makes little sense. Without trust, teachers are more likely to withdraw to the privacy of their own classrooms and repeat past practices, even if they clearly do not work, making improvements in the quality of schooling very unlikely (Bryk and Schneider 2002). Instead, to improve quality in teaching and learning, there must, at the heart, be trust in and nurturing of those who can make the difference (O'Leary 2017). The goal is to use observation to help leaders reignite creativity, innovation, and learning by rehumanizing education (Brown 2012). Subsequent chapters will continue to detail ways to build trusting relationships with teachers using your understanding of vulnerability, empathy, and emotional intelligence.

Chapter Twelve

Listening and Asking the Questions

Nature dictates that it is virtually impossible to accept advice from someone
unless you feel that that person understands you.—John Gottman

Innovative, risk-taking teacher actions have the greatest effect on improved
teaching and learning and are most likely to occur when teachers feel safe
and trusted. A key way to build trust and help teachers feel safe is by practicing empathy while being an attentive listener. When principals act with empathy, they support the conviction that teacher–principal trust is explained
primarily by principal actions to develop supportive ties that relieve teachers'
sense of vulnerability (Bryk and Schneider 2002).

Because listening matters, this chapter examines elements of good listening that build trust. In addition, the reflective conversation questions are
explored, including what they're designed to do as a whole and individually,
what to look for and write, and how to guide answers, all while working to
build trust.

LISTENING

Teachers feel vulnerable during reflective conversations, so what can observers do when asking the questions to relieve excess vulnerability and develop
trust? Primarily, observers promote trust by listening because true listening
builds strength in other people (Greenleaf 2002). People are good listeners
when they purposefully channel all their best emotional intelligence skills,
like being "nice," engaged, and interested. What else factors into good listening? To be the best listeners possible, adopt and practice the following skills:

Empathy. Listen with empathy and compassion for teachers.

Nonverbal listening cues. Simple things like open body language, making eye contact (not always easy when typing), smiling, nodding, and empathetic mirroring of facial expressions all convey observer interest and build trust.

Verbal listening cues. "Yes," "Okay," "Uh-huh," or any other similar words or utterances when the teacher is answering convey listener interest and understanding.

Paraphrasing, reflecting, clarifying, and summarizing. These variants of checking for understanding convey interest in what the teacher says and demonstrate good listening.

Patience. Allowing the teacher to finish her thoughts before asking questions or responding conveys respect, a trust-building element of good listening.

Being present. Typing answers as the teacher talks actually helps observers stay in the moment and focuses listening.

Being curious and asking questions. Staying curious and asking non-judgmental follow-up questions demonstrates good listening and interest while creating feelings of being valued.

Listen well because principal actions when asking questions have the power to make or break trusting relationships.

ASKING QUESTIONS

The first step in the conversation is asking these questions:

- Observers hear teachers' genuine answers on (1) their pedagogical choices and (2) their reflections on what choices could improve the lesson. When observers speak about the lesson first, the norm in many models, teacher responses tend to be colored by observer statements, often mirroring them, and are not necessarily indicative of actual beliefs.
- A message is sent that (1) teacher voice matters, (2) teachers are active participants in an equal back-and-forth conversation, and (3) reflection on practice is an expected norm.
- A message is sent that the observer is interested in what the teacher says.

What were you doing to help students learn? The initial goal of this question is for teachers to reflect on and name the pedagogical strategies they used while being observed. The deeper goal is development of a growth mindset, one where teachers reflexively reflect on their teaching choices in order to maximize student learning. Teacher answers to this question provide insight into a teacher's toolbox, its size, its variety, and the frequency of the use of strategies. In addition, teacher answers contribute to an understanding of teacher mindset and thought processes on teaching, students, and learning. Over time, because of this question, teachers become more thoughtful in reflecting on strategy choices and the reasons behind their choices. They also develop a keener sense of which choices are most effective in helping students learn the intended targets.

When teachers answer this question, make sure they know it's okay to share the tools used not only during the time of the observation but also during the entire class period. Teachers appreciate being given the opportunity to share their pedagogy from the whole lesson because sometimes they feel that pedagogy used during the time they were observed was not representative of their teaching as a whole. When given the opportunity to share what they were doing before or after a principal's visit, the result is that a worried teacher often feels relieved, thereby building trust.

When new to TBO, even after explaining what you're looking for, it's common for teachers to misunderstand the question. Instead of naming pedagogical tools, some teachers will share a daily agenda of activities or the content of the lesson. Practice patience and guide the teachers toward the right answers. To help, when listening to answers, do your best to type them reframed into pedagogical language. Reframing their language is difficult at first, but with twelve conversations per week, it doesn't take long to become proficient at transforming their words into pedagogy. Next, share their words, reframed as pedagogy, in order to train teachers to think and speak about pedagogical tools when they answer. Finally, check in to make sure they agree with the reframed language that was written.

It is also common for teachers to leave out some strategies, which makes sense because the class was the day before and remembering everything is difficult. In these instances, because you have your notes, remind them of the strategies they have left out. Teachers appreciate that their boss has added information that makes the description of the lesson stronger. They feel that you are working with and for and not against them, which builds trust.

It takes some teachers up to a year to gain an understanding of how to answer this question by naming the pedagogical tools they used. As an observer, exercise patience; continue to reframe, add strategies they missed, support, train, and retrain until teachers get it. Let the desire for long-term growth in teaching drive your actions.

On the other hand, some teachers grasp the pedagogical concept immediately, naming each tool chronologically and in exact terms. You can use their abilities to help other teachers by having them lead a brief professional development session on how to answer this question. It doesn't take long, and it does help guide other teachers.

If you had the opportunity to reteach the lesson, what, if anything, might you do differently? This question gauges and develops teacher self-reflection. It provides insight into the following:

- Teachers' willingness and ability to self-reflect accurately
- How naturally and/or often teachers self-reflect
- How they currently use self-reflection to adjust their teaching
- How well they use formative assessment to differentiate their practice

Knowing how often, how well, and how accurately teachers self-reflect provides valuable information on how best to approach and support teachers with growth suggestions. This question proves valuable because it develops reflective teachers who seek evidence that their teaching may not have been successful, which is an invaluable step in ensuring that the desirable lens of success is in place (Hattie 2008).

Before discussing the specifics of what to look for when teachers answer, it's important to understand this question's inherent challenge. When teachers answer this question, in saying they would take different action, they admit their choice may have been wrong. Saying their teaching would have been better done differently is a vulnerability that creates feelings of uncertainty, risk, and emotional exposure (Brown 2012).

The reality is that teaching is already a daily exercise in vulnerability, which Palmer (2017) depicts perfectly: "I went to class that day grateful for another chance to teach; teaching engages my soul as much as any work I know. But I came home that evening convinced once again that I will never master this baffling vocation. Annoyed with some of my students and embarrassed by my own blunders, I pondered a recurring question: Might it be possible, at my age, to find a new line of work, maybe even something I know how to do?"

So when asking this question, principals must help by practicing empathy, being aware of the already present day-to-day vulnerability that is teaching. Let them know you understand, acknowledging that saying that teaching could have been better done differently is vulnerability. Tell them that saying that they might do something differently doesn't necessarily mean the teaching was wrong. That's not how teaching works; it's way too complicated, and there are too many intangibles to have a pedagogical choice be a matter of only right or wrong. Share with teachers what they already know, that on the days when they nailed it, the same lesson taught the same way might have bombed with another group of students because such is teaching. Share that the same goes in reverse for a lesson that didn't go well. Share the reality of teaching: most days, teachers reflect and feel they can make a tweak here or there; on rare days, they feel they bombed and have to redo everything; and on some days, they know they nailed it.

As an observer, creating an environment where teachers feel safe answering this question is essential. To facilitate professional growth that leads to improved student learning outcomes, teachers must reach a level of comfort, safety, and trust where they assume vulnerability with an optimistic expectation of someone else (Boser 2014). When teachers embrace vulnerability and answer this question honestly, honor their answers with empathy because they are demonstrating their trust in you. Teaching effectively with the variables that the developing minds of children, young and old, provide is difficult. Build trust so that teachers offer honest reflections on what could be done differently, confident that they won't be judged critically.

For an observer, additional actions can be taken to help teachers answer honestly. Some teachers feel compelled to manufacture something wrong because of the inherent power differential of the job positions. After all, you're their boss and have the power to hire and fire. Compliant answers based on fear, though, do no good. To minimize this issue, "if anything" was added to the question. Send teachers the message that you know that sometimes nothing in a lesson requires change and that it's okay for a teacher to say they wouldn't change anything. In making this statement, principals are sending a relationship-building message of support. Share this statement with teachers the first time the question is discussed; it helps.

At the same time, it's fair to ask, "What if teachers say they wouldn't change anything and there was something that could have been done differently and better?" If there is something egregious that interferes with student physical or emotional safety, if the classroom management is so poor that it is severely impacting learning and the teachers seem unaware, then intervene immediately to remedy the situation. Beyond that, there are many other contributing factors to consider in determining the best action to take. One is knowing those teachers and where your relationship with them is in its development. The experience of the teachers is another. The magnitude of the suggestion matters, too. The bottom line is that the effective use of emotional intelligence in reading the situation and using that information to guide decision making often makes the difference between developing or not developing a trusting relationship.

If the teachers are new or you are new to the school, the recommendation is erring on the side of patience and waiting until you are confident that there is sufficient trust for a suggestion to be perceived in a positive way. If the suggestion is minor, consider letting it go because, in aiming for growth, it's often best to reserve suggestions for large-impact areas. If it's not minor but teachers are currently working on growth in another area, jot it down for later in their notes document. Don't overload them.

If a trusting relationship is established and it is an important issue for teachers to work on at this time, strive to ask follow-up questions that lead them to answer the question again, stating the growth area themselves. Although this tack doesn't always work, it is a smoother road when teachers identify their own growth area. Finally, if that step doesn't work, ask them if they want to hear a suggestion. The specifics on how to do so will be discussed in chapter 14.

There are rare times when teachers prove to be consistently unaware of seemingly obvious things that could have been differently. This situation is a sign of a serious problem that has to be dealt with at the appropriate time, and it is explained in chapter 14.

As an observer, listen to teachers' answers without judgment, typing what they say and reframing when necessary. If you disagree that something they said requires a change, tell them. Almost all teachers are self-reflective to some degree; the best ones are often overly self-critical. Don't be afraid to share when self-criticism doesn't seem accurate. Doing so builds trust.

The Question of the Year. This question supports schoolwide professional development for a year on a targeted growth area where most teachers have room for growth. Whether this area is decided by a district, a division principal, an entire leadership team, or teachers and principals together doesn't matter. It is a chance for an entire faculty collectively to grow their skills in a common area.

Although most teachers require professional development in the target area, some don't, which provides an amazing opportunity. Those that don't are your in-house experts, and they will be equally involved. They will play an instrumental role in leading and supporting the targeted professional development area, guiding the growth of their peers. Since teaching others is the highest form of learning, these teachers receive the benefit of becoming even better at that particular pedagogical area, and, even better, they are becoming empowered teacher leaders, which is another relationship builder.

For teachers, being asked regularly about their progress with the question of the year serves as an effective accountability measure. As a teacher, purposeful professional development that is worked on schoolwide, combined with the knowledge that they are going to be regularly asked about their progress, does wonders to push pedagogical growth forward. The use of this question has really made a difference in improving teacher skills in specific pedagogical areas.

What progress have you made toward your action research big goal? It's important to explain what action research is before discussing the question's function. Everyone is familiar with setting annual goals. TBO adds a specific data comparison action research measure to pedagogy improvement goals. Doing so develops researcher mindsets, where classrooms become experimentation labs and teachers determine the effect of new strategies on student performance.

Action research big goals begin as teachers make decisions on a new pedagogical strategy or significant tweak to strategy that they plan to add to their practice. The standard SMART goal template (specific, measurable, attainable, relevant, timed) works well for developing their target. As teachers create their goal, the specifics of the measurement comparison, the "M" of SMART, is crucial in determining the success of their initiative. It's important that teachers find an effective comparative measure to determine whether their new strategy improves achievement. Successful measurement examples include any or all of the following:

- Comparing unit final assessment scores from the same unit the previous year
- Comparing final assessment scores from a previous unit the same year
- Comparing consecutive district interim formative progress assessment scores

Comparative measurements of student performance are an effective way to determine the impact that teachers' concentrated efforts at improving an area of pedagogy have on learning outcomes.

Some teachers struggle initially with developing these measurements. Often, the reason is that they are used to a goal-setting model that might aim for something like 75 percent of students achieving 80 percent or higher on the final assessment for a particular unit or academic year. Explain that the goal is determining the effectiveness of the new strategy by comparing student performance outcomes using the new pedagogical strategy with student performance outcomes before the strategy was implemented. In the 75 percent example, the problem is that there is no comparison to teaching before the new strategy was implemented, meaning there is no formative information for teachers on the role the new strategy played in student performance. By instead comparing scores to another assessment before the implementation of the strategy, there is direct comparative evidence of whether the strategy affected student performance.

As a general rule, let teachers choose their own goal, but there are exceptions. One is when teachers' lack of self-awareness on their growth areas interfere with improvement. For example, a teacher struggling with classroom management chooses a goal related to feedback. While feedback is an excellent area to work on, without basic classroom management, not much learning of any type will occur. In these situations, guide the teacher to choose a more impactful goal: classroom management in this example. Another exception is when a teacher is on an improvement plan and principal input is crucial to chances for teacher improvement.

Over the course of the year, teachers monitor and measure progress while observer and teacher discuss impact and develop adjustments as necessary during reflective conversations. Whether the new strategy works as predicted doesn't matter. Not all new strategies will work out as well as planned. The new information gleaned from the attempt matters, as does broadening teacher skill sets. Developing risk-taking growth mindsets matters most of all. The action research big goal question serves two main functions:

1. Its design provides a supportive element of accountability for teachers' big pedagogical goal. When teachers know they will be asked regularly and frequently about the progress of their goal, it stays in the forefront of their minds, and therefore their actions are more ardently driven by achieving their goal. The question works as an intermittent reinforcement accountability tool in the sense that teachers know that an observation is coming, but don't know exactly when. Most teachers appreciate having accountability built into the process.

2. It allows for regular and supportive feedback on the progress of the new practice that serves as the teachers' big goal. When teachers take risks and innovate by adding or substantially changing an area of their teaching, they are often reluctant to persist in implementing the new practice in the absence of evidence that what they're doing makes a positive difference. Often when doing something new, there is an implementation dip before there is forward progress. In the absence of principal support and feedback in the face of these perceived failures, a teacher will ultimately tend to press back into familiar and "safer" modes of teaching (Cogan 1973). Therefore, it's important to build some mechanism into the implementation process to show teachers that these new practices are working (Guskey 2014) or to provide supportive suggestions for possible adjustment to the use of the strategy. This question serves as the mechanism that encourages teachers to persist in the face of potential struggles.

When principals engage in reflective conversations regularly, they are able to share that it's normal for things to get worse initially before overall improvement is experienced. Knowing that things can get worse before they improve is important. When teachers understand the struggles that can accompany new efforts and know they are supported by their principals while working through these struggles, it is much easier to persevere until success is achieved. When principals understand the normal process for implementation of a new strategy, they are allowed to show greater empathy and patience while supporting teacher growth, again a huge relationship builder that leads to improved teaching and learning.

Is there anything specific you would like me to look for on the next visit? Is there anything else you would like me to add to the form? These final questions, the only ones asked at the end of the reflective conversation, have proven to be an important part of the relationship-building process. Asking the first question demonstrates a desire on the part of principals to make sure they are working to meet the needs of teachers. It demonstrates a genuine interest in seeing if there is anything specific principals can do to support teachers.

The second question ensures that communication is clear and well understood by both parties. Again, just asking this question has shown itself to be another demonstration that principals care about what teachers think and feel, and therefore the question works to build a trusting relationship between teachers and principals.

Chapter Thirteen

Sharing "Evidence Of"

The heart of valuable feedback is taking the strengths perspective.—Brene Brown

The reflective conversation began by asking questions while listening intently to and writing down teachers' answers. The next step is letting teachers know the details of the different areas of teaching you noticed. In TBO sharing, evidence of observed teaching functions as a sharing of strengths designed to build trust, enhance teachers' awareness of their practice, and build capacity. The heart of valuable feedback is taking the "strengths perspective." Viewing performance from the strengths perspective offers the opportunity to examine struggles in light of capacities, talents, competencies, possibilities, visions, values, and hopes (Brown 2012). By focusing on strengths, there is a smoother path to improvement. It allows teachers to consider positive qualities as potential resources (Brown 2012).

Teachers like hearing about their strengths; even when they were embarrassed, they still wanted to hear appreciation verbalized (Rosenberg 2015). Focusing on strengths works; when positive aspects of performance are emphasized, self-efficacy is enhanced along with aspirations, efficient analytical thinking, and self-satisfaction, and this often leads to enhanced performance (O'Leary 2017).

As you begin sharing "Evidence of," always tell teachers to let you know if something they did well wasn't noticed. Sharing this statement is a relationship builder. Also, when sharing evidence, prefacing what was observed by using the words "I noticed . . ." has been shown to be an effective way for teachers to internalize the evidence being shared as positive, which is a more powerful enforcer of their teaching.

Beginning with the learning targets (LTs) and working through all the areas on the form, what follows are suggestions on what and how to share evidence with teachers.

Learning Targets (LTs). As previously discussed, there is no way to see all the LT criteria during a twenty-minute observation. It takes time to witness all areas and gain a full picture of teacher effectiveness using LTs. In the beginning, when sharing what LT areas were noticed, it pays to explain. Sharing that there is no expectation to see all the areas helps ease teacher worries about unchecked boxes, thereby building a sense of safety for them. Teachers do worry, so sharing this information helps build teacher comfort in the reflective conversations.

During most observations, one is likely to see if the target is written properly, constantly displayed, and formatively assessed. Other areas depend on which portion of the class was observed. Share the areas you observed. Even if an area that ought to have been observed wasn't seen, don't comment on it. Commenting on a missing area only serves to interfere with the trust-building process. This statement holds true whether the conversation occurs early in the relationship or once it is more established. There will be time for growth suggestions later.

The table's checkboxes make clear the expectations for LTs. Often as you are sharing what was noticed, teachers will realize they left an area out. Sometimes they will comment on their omission and let you know they will add it next time. Even if they don't comment on it, teachers often realize their mistake and make the changes on their own. They do it because an expectation listed on the form was left blank. Teachers often make adjustments without a suggestion because the form sends a message.

When teachers make comments about not using an LT area and their plan to fix it next time, it generally works best to acknowledge that sometimes these things happen and ask if they want any help adding this LT area to practice. Sometimes it was a mistake. Sometimes it was part of their learning curve. Either way, when teachers are being reflective enough to mention it, any comments besides these are likely to work against a great growth opportunity.

Risk Taking/Innovative Practice. Notes can be written here when you clearly notice teachers attempting a new practice, but it is not necessary. The main point, as already mentioned, is as a visual reminder to tell teachers how much risk taking is valued. Teachers are welcome to tell you something on which they were taking a risk. Write it down when they do.

Teacher–Student Rapport and Relationship and Classroom and Student Behavior Management. These two areas are fairly straightforward; just share the specific strategies and interactions that were noticed. Use the terminology of toolbox possibilities and definitely share dialogue that was relevant.

An important point on sharing evidence of relationship and management is that these are the two categories where you are most likely to observe a bias or equity issue. When you see a teacher guilty of a bias or equity issue with a student or group of students, be it conscious or unconscious, the immediate temptation is to type about and comment on the area of concern—rightfully so, considering the urgency that correcting bias and equity issues is finally being given. Keeping in line with the strengths and relationship focus of TBO, these notes are typically pushed to the bottom of the form or put in the teacher's notes document to be discussed and worked on later. Unless it is an egregious example or an overtly conscious teacher action, especially when you are new and building relationships, waiting is probably still a good idea. However, because correcting this mistake is an urgent matter, the recommendation is to address it as soon as possible with the teacher.

On the flip side, whenever you see an example of teachers avoiding or eliminating a previous equity or bias issue or see them purposefully working to be more inclusive, be sure to share the noticed efforts with the teachers. Sharing that positive example works wonders in improving their cognizance of bias and equity issues and actions, further improving teachers' ability to notice times when these issues might interfere with student progress. Awareness is a powerful tool in changing action.

Cooperative Learning. Without a doubt, collaborative learning done properly is one of the most effective tools students can engage in to positively impact their learning. Reinforce teacher use of the strategy by sharing the name of the cooperative learning structures observed and hopefully the Xs, showing that the activity included each area of PIES: positive interdependence, individual accountability, equal participation, and simultaneous interaction. Since all the structures are designed to include each area, the likelihood is that all four boxes will be marked, and therefore it is an easy way to share a teacher win.

It can also be helpful to contrast the increase in student engagement in cooperative activities compared to a more traditional classroom lesson. Share examples of student interactions that you observed, use dialogue, and contrast with a more traditional activity. Highlight the peer formative assessment actions that allow students to correct mistakes immediately versus a traditional model where a student would keep perpetuating mistakes.

Working Memory: 10-2 Reflection and Processing Time. Sharing feedback on working memory is another area where the form does most of the work for you. Show teachers the times when activities and reflection activities began and remind them of the activities. If a teacher has left out reflection activities, there is no need to say anything. The form does it for you. Having "reflection activity" on the table does wonders in helping teachers purposefully incorporate them into their practice. The same goes for the working memory theory of ten minutes. There is no need to comment on activities that last longer than ten minutes. The table sends the message. If teachers comment on their activity lasting too long, it works well to send a message of support, letting them know that by just noticing the length of their activities, you know they will be working on getting better at stopping sooner to provide processing time.

As teacher skills progress in using working memory effectively, shortening learning activities, and adding reflection activities, highlight the growth. It's even better when you can share student processing dialogue supporting new or deeper learning.

Some teachers are resistant to honoring working memory and adding reflection activities to their practice. They fear that the time it takes to complete the activities, which can really be two minutes per activity, takes valuable time away from getting their content in. In these instances, share working memory research on improved retention of student learning, which allows the class to move faster because more of them get it, thus reducing time spent reteaching.

Questioning and Higher-Order Thinking. Again, the table demonstrates expectations for good practice, which makes it easy to share evidence without being negative. The inverted pyramid does the talking, allowing teachers to self-assess potential growth areas without feeling like their boss is being critical of them.

It's best to begin sharing feedback in the questions section by letting teachers know that the expectation is that in the course of most lessons, it's normal and appropriate to ask questions at all different levels on the pyramid. Share that the goal is to be cognizant and purposeful with questions, working toward asking more higher-order thinking questions that push and lead students to greater depths of learning and understanding. Be sure to also share that you do your best to place the questions in the appropriate category but mistakenly place a question in the wrong area once in a while. Admitting this reality prevents more skeptical teachers from discounting what you say with a "gotcha" moment. Let teachers know that it's okay for them to ask that a question be moved to a higher category if they feel that is where it belongs. Sharing this information builds trust.

As an observer, share the details for each question asked: think time prior to looking for answers, how many students answered the questions, and the actual question that was asked. Generally, when teachers see a variety of levels, they feel pretty good about their use of questions. Sometimes they will see the majority of their questions at the lower levels and will comment on that. Again, as soon as they have commented on where their questions are located, progress is being made; they are self-assessing. It's best to tell them it's okay—one lesson does not form an opinion—and see if they would like support on improving their use of questioning.

Share when you see improvements in providing greater think time, in having all students answer, and in greater depth of questions. When warranted, keep those affirmations flowing.

Formative assessment, feedback, and differentiation often work in conjunction with and feed off one another. Often, sharing evidence in formative assessments leads to teacher reflection or to teacher next steps with feedback and differentiation. Cognizance of these connections helps observers when sharing "Evidence of" in these categories.

Formative Assessment/Knowing What Each Student Has Learned to Guide Next Steps. The table on the observation form sets out the range of methods for formatively assessing each student's learning. Let the form do the work and just share the information on each formative assessment that was noticed. Share who did the assessing, how it was done, and the type. If more was noticed, share those details, too. Just the act of sharing what was noticed often leads to teachers telling observers more about what they did with the information received, things like providing descriptive progress feedback to students, making adjustments to their plans, and differentiating instruction based on each student's results. When teachers don't share what they did with the information, follow-up questions can be used to guide growth in this area, which will be addressed in chapter 14.

With time, a picture of overall formative assessment use and ability will emerge. The frequency and effectiveness of teachers' use of formative assessment varies greatly; overall, its use to guide next steps is not as strong as is desired. The good news is that because all teachers practice some "in-the-moment" formative assessment, you are able to share some "Evidence of," even if only at a basic level. Noticing evidence at any level aids greatly in serving as a starting point to work from on the path to helping build teacher skills in this or any area.

Descriptive Progress Feedback. This is the perfect place to point out the importance of modeling good practice. If you can't walk the talk giving feedback during reflective conversations, then teachers lose respect for you, greatly reducing your ability to affect teacher growth. Avoid the hypocrisy between the way most observation models give feedback to teachers and the way teachers are expected to give feedback to students. Instead, model good teacher-to-student feedback practice: provide nonevaluative, strengths-based, positive feedback that aims to build teacher self-efficacy.

As with formative assessment, the table lays out the range of ways that feedback can be provided. Begin by sharing the descriptive progress feedback details for every time it was noticed. Share who gave the feedback and the type: basic, instructional, or coaching. Add the specifics of the feedback conversations. Sharing these specific scripted words, teacher to student and student to student, can be a powerful tool in influencing teacher effectiveness.

Being able to share any evidence of practice is always a good place to start. The good news is that all teachers provide informal feedback to students, so finding evidence of some strength in this area is easy. Over time, because the table lays out expectations for the variety of ways descriptive progress feedback can be given, teachers tend to work toward increasing their use of currently underutilized ways of giving feedback.

Specific Differentiation. The table, like so many others, lays out teacher expectations for the ways teachers can differentiate, ranging from the method (intuitive or intentional), the area (content, process, or product), and the learner voice accessed (readiness, interest, or preference). Begin by sharing the details of each time differentiated teacher practice was noticed. Add any relevant specific details that add insight.

At first, it will be common to observe mostly intuitive differentiation. The good news is that almost all teachers differentiate intuitively, so there will be some evidence you notice, which is the best way to build further skill development. Noticing intuitive differentiation cannot be overstated because other areas of differentiation are often challenging for teachers to build into practice. Over time, because the table lays out expectations, teachers tend to advance their practice, being more purposeful and planning their differentiation. The evidence you share will grow in depth as skills develop.

Some elements of differentiation can be challenging for observers to identify in practice; you don't know the students as well as the teacher; you don't know the details of how that particular class functions. Since it is difficult to notice, let teachers know that you want them to share if differentiation activities occurred but weren't written about. You want to build trust and to have everything positive that occurred in class be noted.

Learning Principles Used. It's important to begin by pointing out to teachers that the list of their activities written in the table is a representation of only twenty minutes of one lesson. Let them know there are times that it's appropriate to use activities that fit in all of the different learning principle levels and that a mix is fine; over time, the goal is to have more of the activities in the bottom, more active and generally impactful half of the pyramid. Let them know that some activities are more difficult to place accurately on the form and that if they feel something was placed inaccurately to let you know.

Other than sharing those statements, just show them the table and make any comments on it that you wish. They are free to tell you other activities that occurred before or after your visit if that helps ease any potential worries they might have or to provide a clearer picture of the entire lesson. Teachers will see where their activities are located on the table, and if the range of their activities could use adjustment, the table frequently does a good job of sending the message without you having to say anything judgmental or negative. Improvement over time is the norm.

Student Interview. Sharing student answers to the questions with teachers functions much like a forced formative assessment activity, providing valuable information on how well student learning aligns with desired teaching. The answers provide insight for individual lessons, but more important, over time, they provide a holistic picture of levels of alignment.

The best thing to do is to tell the teachers what the students said and not judge one way or the other. Know that there will be occasions when all the interviewed students will be the ones who normally struggle, even when the lesson and teaching were highly impressive, just like there will be times when the students who always get it were asked and the targets weren't as clear. Sometimes teachers will protest that the students asked were the ones who usually struggle. Acknowledge their belief (it probably is true), and it builds trust. No matter what the student answers are, the information is great for differentiation discussions. Remind teachers that each lesson observed is a snapshot and not a judgment. When there is no alignment, teachers worry; share that the information isn't about right or wrong.

Teaching Intangibles, Scripting, Questions, Suggestions, and Additional Pedagogy. Sharing these extras—especially the intangibles, specific scripted statements, and additional pedagogy—has often proven to be a valuable relationship builder that has spurred further teacher risk taking. Whatever positive evidence you noticed that belongs here, share it and celebrate it with teachers. Something caught your attention that was impressive. Let them know.

For questions or suggestions, sometimes it is best to move them to the teacher's notes document for later. Let intuition guide you. Even if something will be brought up, it works best to have a number of lines of separation between the questions, suggestions, and positives you noticed. It lessens the chances of distraction; you want them to hear evidence of good practice.

TROUBLESHOOTING ADDITIONAL OBSERVER QUESTIONS ON SHARING EVIDENCE

What do you do, though, when you aren't seeing many strengths yet you know how important it is to build relationship by sharing evidence? Sometimes with more traditional and with new teachers, this situation presents itself. First, if learning is not going on or the environment is not safe, jump in right away to try to help improve things. Build relationships later.

Strive to create an empathetic environment, though, one where teachers feel you are working with and not against them. It really is about empathy; the teacher doesn't want to be in the current situation, probably knows it's bad, feels awful, and is full of anxiety because teaching is not going well. Be supportive and encouraging while working to build a better classroom.

Other times, though, when the class is safe and teaching is occurring, it can be difficult to find evidence of good practice aligned with the observation form. In these times, there are creative ways to share evidence of strengths in a genuine way. Don't manufacture things; rather, look outside the limits of the form to find evidence of strengths. Maybe a lecture demonstrates excellent content knowledge, maybe a teacher's attempts at jokes demonstrate excellent effort toward building relationships, maybe it's clear the teacher has put in a lot of time planning, or maybe there is an incremental improvement over the previous visit. There are ways, and there is evidence to be seen; find it. These situations are common enough to know that it pays to get creative. Sharing evidence of strengths, no matter the minimal degree, builds relationships and factors into teachers' willingness to work with you later and take risks to grow their practice.

What about when you see expertise that could be used to help other teachers improve their skills in that area? What a super problem to have. First, share with teachers the expertise you see. Second, begin planting seeds that will hopefully lead to teachers sharing their excellence and leading professional development for other teachers at school. Further steps on what to do with teaching expertise will be discussed in chapter 19.

Chapter Fourteen

Offering Suggestions

People are desperate for feedback—we all want to grow. We just need to learn how to give feedback in a way that inspires growth and engagement.—Brene Brown

A significant problem interfering with traditional post-observation conference success is the complete dichotomy between the way teachers are supposed to give feedback to students and the norms for the ways observers are supposed to give feedback to teachers. The actions in both situations ought to be the same, but they aren't. When comparing feedback best practice guidelines between teachers to students and observers to teachers, the differences paint a stark contrast.

Effective feedback to students points out strengths; is nonevaluative, actionable, timely, and ongoing; doesn't give too much information; offers suggestions instead of advice; limits corrective information to an amount the student can act on; and builds self-efficacy (Chappuis 2012; Fleischer et al. 2013; Wiggins 2012). In contrast, when generalizing the norms of the most prevalent models of observation, feedback to teachers consists of evaluatively rating teachers on an inordinately large number of pedagogical areas, is not timely for formal observations, and is infrequent. The evaluative nature of feedback, combined with the enormity of the ratings categories, often paralyzes teachers, frequently causing them to wonder where to begin and definitely interfering with self-efficacy.

Feedback practices for observers to teachers are more effective when they mirror teacher-to-student feedback practices, which is what TBO aims to do. It points out strengths, is nonevaluative, limits the areas of pedagogy to a manageable number, and is timely. Suggestions for growth are limited to one major area at a time, and observers offer continuous support and resources for growth, thereby building teacher self-efficacy.

There are a number of areas to take into account when offering suggestions. All increase the likelihood that teachers will embrace suggestions.
These areas include the following:

- Preparation—doing the prep work physically and mentally (your mind-
  set)
- What and how much to suggest
- Words matter, or the "how-to" of offering suggestions, the dos and don'ts,
- Explaining what continuing support looks like and entails
- Troubleshooting potential suggestion issues

WHEN TO OFFER SUGGESTIONS

TBO requires sharing "evidence of" strengths only for the first three visits;
therefore, the earliest time to offer suggestions is at the fourth reflective
conversation. As previously discussed, exceptions are made in cases involv-
ing student safety or where management issues prevent the class from learning. Even if you already know your teachers when you begin using TBO,
send a powerful message about the new, more teacher-friendly way of doing
things by honoring the rule. Focus on building relationships and taking actions that honor the time they take to develop; view practice with a focus on
strengths as opposed to ratings. It pays dividends. By waiting, teachers will
see and respect a new you, which is especially true if previous actions and
practice were significantly different from TBO. Waiting pays dividends.

Besides the fourth-visit rule, other factors to consider in determining
when to offer suggestions are teacher experience and principal perception of
teacher readiness and mindset. Generally, younger and newer teachers tend
to be more open and ready for suggestions; they also tend to be the ones with
the most room for growth. On the flip side, as most principals know, there
can be a tendency for experienced teachers to be comfortable with the skills
they have developed, and therefore they can be more resistant to change. And
yes, to be clear, there are and always will be experienced teachers who
continually possess a growth mindset just like there are and always will be
younger teachers who tend toward more a fixed mindset.

The best advice related to these generalizations is to let your intuition
guide you, but when in doubt, wait to offer suggestions. You will find that
the reflective conversations tell you a lot. Teachers' tone of voice, open or
closed body language, and words will help in ascertaining how open teachers
are to receiving suggestions. The good news is that when you offer only
"evidence of" strengths first, a surprising number of teachers will ask what
they can get better at, even after only one or two visits. Despite the request,
don't give them suggestions yet. Experience has shown that between 70 and

80 percent of teachers will ask for suggestions by the end of the third reflective conversation. At this point, observers know that these teachers are on board, relationships have been established, and teachers are beginning to trust and feel safe. Observers can comfortably begin offering suggestions to these teachers after the fourth visit; such is the power of initially focusing only on "evidence of" strengths.

So, generally, it is the other 20 percent for whom the "when" has to be determined. With the teachers who haven't asked what they can get better at, it's usually easier to offer supported suggestions earlier to newer teachers without fear of interfering with relationships. It's generally wiser to proceed more cautiously with more experienced teachers. Beyond this broad advice, it really does come down to intuition combined with differentiation. Trust that you will get a feel for your teachers, but when you are not sure that they are ready, wait.

As an added factor working in a principal's favor, often the energy of so many teachers taking risks on new pedagogical areas will pull others along as well. They don't want to be left out, so they decide to try out something new, too. One teacher the author worked with saw all the other teachers in his department change to team seating arrangements as they began incorporating cooperative learning into their practice and so changed his seating as well so as not to be the odd one out. He was now ready, and the next reflective conversation included a supported suggestion on adding cooperative learning into practice.

There is a limit on how long to wait; the maximum time is one year. That might sound crazy, but when playing the long game, it can pay off. Since observers know to take action in egregious or poor classroom management situations, continuing with less than ideal for a while longer actually helps if it improves the odds for growth. The two most common situations where waiting this long makes sense are with teachers who seem extremely afraid of change, usually veteran teachers, and if your school has had a history of observations that have been evaluative and critical. When you change your style, it will take some people longer to let go of the past ways, to trust, and to open themselves up to the new you and the new way.

After practicing TBO for one year, though, it's fair to offer suggestions to even the most reluctant teacher. One year is more than enough time to demonstrate trust and that your interest is in teachers and their growth.

Two valuable lessons learned while practicing TBO are that there are nearly limitless ways for teachers to demonstrate teaching excellence and that it can pay to wait on suggestions. These lessons were almost learned the hard way. As a new principal in a school, I observed a veteran teacher with twenty-five years of experience multiple times. The content knowledge was incredibly strong, but the pedagogy seemed so traditional, lots of chalk and talk, and the teacher seemed really strict. I was uncomfortable with the teaching and wanted to offer a suggestion after the fourth visit, but something told me to wait.

While waiting, I discovered that this teacher's International Baccalaureate scores, year in and year out, were well over one and a quarter points above the world average. Now I found myself watching him with the perspective of what was working. The more I observed, the more I noticed strengths that weren't apparent before. His accountability bar for his students was as high as I had ever seen. The organizational tools he shared with his students, along with his seemingly breakneck pace, kept them focused and on track; his dry sense of humor played really well with his students. As this "Evidence of" good teaching was noticed, it became apparent that what he was doing could really help other teachers. So instead of offering a suggestion, I asked him to put on a professional development session for our faculty. He was reluctant, calling himself a dinosaur, but with persistence he eventually agreed. After the presentation, titled "Jurassic Thinking 101," more than half a dozen teachers thanked him for giving them permission to be more demanding with their students.

Imagine what could have happened if I had made suggestions for growth too early. Maybe I wouldn't have discovered his strengths. Maybe he would have pulled back, grown unhappy knowing how successful his students performed in International Baccalaureate, and sought to move to another school. We certainly know that his peers and therefore all the students in the school would not have benefited from his strengths being shared with all the teachers.

Practice patience, bite your tongue, and fight the sometimes overwhelming urge to want to fix things right away. Offering suggestions right away will interfere with the development of the desired trusting relationship. Some observers will say, "But they asked what they can get better at." It doesn't matter—being patient and building relationship supersede all else. If they ask for advice before the fourth visit, tell them that you are taking your time getting to know them. Even if you already know them and their teaching, tell them that you are taking a new look and want to be patient before offering suggestions.

PREPARATION

There are two areas of preparation: physical and mental. The physical preparation is necessary for every suggestion; it is doing the homework necessary in order to guide the teacher toward success. The mental part is necessary when there is a likelihood of resistance to the suggestion; it is preparing yourself for these responses.

As an instructional leader, being prepared to offer specific guided support for the growth suggestion is an absolute. Create a plan for the teacher and come armed; the depth of the plan depends on the teacher. Some teachers will not require much beyond the suggestion, and others will require a fairly detailed plan of support. Use your experience with each teacher, combined with your intuition, to guide you.

If there are articles or books to recommend from the TBO Web links, be prepared to share and discuss them. If outside professional development training is going to be offered, have all the information ready. If there is an in-house expert with whom the teacher can work, make sure everything is lined up with the expert teacher. Whatever the plan, have all the tools at the ready during the conversation. Being prepared and offering specific methods or plans to support growth serve a dual purpose: providing support tools maximizes the chances of growth, and, beyond modeling good practice, it sends a message of care that fosters teacher risk taking.

Uncomfortable feelings of fear will arise before preparing to offer suggestions to teachers you think will be resistant; dealing with that is the mental part. It's normal for the brain to jump into fight-or-flight mode and anticipate a negative conversation. The brain is sending that message to protect you. However, the likelihood that the outcome will be the same as the message that the brain is warning you about is incredibly small. The details of this phenomenon will be discussed in chapter 18. In the meantime, understand what the brain is doing; don't let it prevent you from taking action. Ways to prepare include the following:

- Anticipate what teachers' negative responses might be and preplan responses to their response.
- Tell yourself that the mind's feared outcomes are not likely. The more often you engage in these potentially difficult conversations, the easier it is to experientially know that the mind is trying to protect you and that the chances of a bad conversation are slim.
- Seek the feedback of a peer or mentor. You have to be willing to ask for and receive feedback in order to be good at giving it. The truth is that sometimes the size, severity, or complexity of a problem doesn't always reflect the emotional reactivity to it. A peer can help observers get to the same side of the table as the teacher so that they can be present and therefore be much more likely to see the change that's requested (Brown 2012).
- Practice by role-playing the conversation if you are really worried about the outcome.

Brown (2012) sums it up clearly: giving and soliciting feedback is about learning and growth, and understanding who we are and how we respond to the people around us is the foundation in this process. Victory is taking off the armor, showing up, and engaging.

WHAT AND HOW MUCH TO SUGGEST

It's easy to feel compelled to find some area for teachers to improve in during every observation. Anyone looking hard enough can find an area where someone can improve. It's important to ask yourself what the potential learning benefits are from focusing on something every time. Choosing to spend time making suggestions every visit will work against what you are building. Strengths you share won't be heard, teachers will feel picked on, and teachers will feel overloaded. The trust that is necessary to take risks will not be established. So, what is worthy of a suggestion? Big strategies, ones that will have the largest impact on improved student learning.

Regarding how much to suggest, remember the teacher is already working on a big pedagogical action research goal and that the whole school is working on the question-of-the-year area. As instructional coaching guru Jim Knight discovered in his coaching work, "One common theme that emerged is the importance of focusing on one goal at a time" (Knight et al. 2015). Both research on effective practices and teacher perception of best practices offer support for this approach. When a coach works to implement too many practices at once, teachers become overwhelmed, and practice does not change. He found that the most successful coaches offered sustained support on a limited number of high-leverage strategies (Knight 2009). So, aside from a little quick fix, the best success will likely transpire when one major area is worked on at a time. Depending on the teacher, the annual big goal might be that one, while others can do another. Let your intuition guide you as to the best move for each teacher.

WORDS MATTER: HOW TO OFFER SUGGESTIONS

Suggestions are received more positively when you use the right words. Use the wrong words, phrasing, and/or tone, and teachers will have a tendency to retreat into a more protective place and resist the suggestion. Use the right words and say them in a nonthreatening way, where teachers feel they have some choice, and they tend to be more willing to embrace the growth opportunity.

To know what words to use, it makes sense to begin with the words and phrases not to use. Some words almost automatically create resistance because they threaten people's inherent desire for autonomy. When people hear a demand, they tend to resist because it threatens their desire for self-determination, their independence. Words or phrases that create negative feelings or that deny a feeling of choice include *should, have to, need,* and *supposed to.* All imply that there is no choice (Rosenberg 2015). So to increase chances of success when offering suggestions to teachers, TBO recommends taking these words out of your suggestion vocabulary.

Knowing what not to say, what words can be used that offer the best chance that teachers will embrace a suggestion? The following prefaces have proven successful in engaging cooperation:

- Would you be willing to . . . ? (Rosenberg 2015)
- May I share a suggestion?
- I have a favor; would you like to hear what it is?
- I have a suggestion; would you be interested in hearing?
- Would you mind if I offered a suggestion?

In contrasting these similar phrases with what not to say, the difference is clear. The observer is asking for permission to even share the suggestion. In asking for permission, the teacher has the right to say no; there is no demand. Just the act of asking permission causes people to be much more willing to embrace the suggestion. It seems so simple and almost defies logic, but semantics make that much difference. Ask before offering advice (Rosenberg 2015). A couple of other ideas on how to offer suggestions include the following:

- Focus on what you want rather than what you don't want. Talk about what one doesn't want to talk about creates resistance among conflicting parties (Rosenberg 2015).
- Confess to having made the same mistake when you were a teacher; this increases the likelihood that the teacher will accept the comments (Marshall 2013).

Once the teacher has committed to hearing and then accepting the growth suggestion (the reality in more than 90 percent of cases), preparation comes into play. You share your support plan and work through the details with the teacher.

EXPLAINING WHAT CONTINUING SUPPORT LOOKS LIKE AND ENTAILS

Once suggestions have been shared with teachers, the next step is explaining the support they can expect to receive. Support plays a crucial role in fostering growth, and the TBO model of continuously cycling through observations with teachers adds to the ability to provide support because the feedback is ongoing (Knight 2015). So let teachers know that they can expect to engage in continuing supportive conversations on the progress being made with the implementation.

As teachers work to grow by implementing or tweaking new strategies, it's invaluable to let them know that there can often be an implementation dip causing difficulties when trying something new (Fullan 2002). The reality is that teachers who are trying to develop new classroom competencies generally require continuing in-class support to be successful. Without such help, the failures that teachers almost always experience in attempts to change established behavior will ultimately tend to press them back into familiar, "safer" modes of teaching (Cogan 1973).

For teachers and administrators, knowing that things can go backward before they improve is essential for sustained growth. This knowledge helps ease teacher worries, knowing that it can be a normal part of the process for things to go backward and get worse initially before overall improvement is experienced. When teachers know that observers understand this phenomenon and will support them through these struggles, it is much easier for teachers to persevere. A knowledge of dips in implementation heightens the importance of observers continuously being in classes and lending support when teachers can benefit most from it. The last thing anyone wants is for teachers to revert to safer but less productive behaviors.

Also let teachers know that they are welcome to invite observers anytime to get feedback on their new practice. When teachers feel safe asking their supervisor to watch them, be it to share a breakthrough moment or to get advice on a struggle or dip, success is much more likely to ensue. Let teachers know they are free to ask to observe others or ask for anything they think will help them get better with their new or improved pedagogical strategy.

TROUBLESHOOTING CHALLENGES TO OFFERS OF SUGGESTIONS

When trusting relationships have been built and discretion is used in deciding when to offer suggestions, resistance is rare. On occasion, though, issues surrounding suggestions arise.

What if teachers ask what they can get better at before you are ready? This common occurrence is a good problem to have. Most teachers want to get better at their jobs, and most also want to please their boss. These two factors work together often in the form of teachers asking for feedback early in the TBO process.

As stated previously, there is a strong likelihood that during any observation, there will be things that observers notice that could be improved. Despite this, building trusting relationships comes first, and that means waiting, even when teachers ask before the fourth visit. It truly does take time to get to know teachers' teaching; by sharing that you are still getting to know their teaching, you are sending a message of respect that definitely builds trust. Even if you already know your teachers, by waiting, you are demonstrating that you are taking a new, more patient approach, which also builds trust. Let them know you'll offer a suggestion in time.

What if teachers resist the feedback suggestions? This is less common, but it does happen. There are two general ways for resistance to transpire. One is simply saying no to the question, asking if you can offer a suggestion. The other is when teachers resist the area of suggestion and instead offer a different area for them to work on improving.

Again, it proves useful to first explain what not to do. The goal is engaging cooperation and building trust. The following actions will work directly against these goals:

- E-mailing feedback and suggestions. Absolutely the worst tactic to take is e-mailing feedback. Suggestions are usually e-mailed when observers feel super busy and are trying to save time, when they are afraid of potential conflicts, or when it is the design of model. E-mailing feedback builds walls, not bridges. Don't do it!
- Using the authority of the supervisor position to engage cooperation. This action treads into the category of demands and will not result in genuine engagement. There are rare occasions when using positional authority makes sense, but now is not that time.
- Getting teachers to go along by telling them all you've done for them. Guilting someone into compliance will destroy relationships with all teachers, not just one.

The best advice on what to do if teachers resist the growth suggestion—whether by not wanting to hear or by offering their own suggestions instead—is to show an empathic understanding of what prevents those from doing as we asked. That does not mean to give up when teachers say no to the request. It means to not engage in persuasion until you have empathized with what's preventing them person from saying yes (Rosenberg 2015). Empathizing does help engage cooperation—often the next time you ask, they will accept.

At times, teacher feelings of disengagement are the issue underlying the resistance. Disengagement takes many forms: people disengage to protect themselves from vulnerability, shame, and feeling lost and without purpose. People also disengage when they feel like the people who are leading them aren't living up to their end of the social contract (Brown 2012). With time and trust, the chances of engaging the teacher to work through the resistance increase.

When it comes down to the decision of whether to go with the suggestion of the teacher or your own, it often pays dividends to accept the teacher's suggestion. Doing so now increases the likelihood that the teacher will embrace your suggestion the next time. It also sends a trust message. There will be times when you feel strongly that it is better to work on your suggestion first, usually because not doing so interferes with basic student learning. In these situations, explain the rationale honestly and then go for it.

FINAL THOUGHTS

To develop and sustain continuous success, teachers must make changes because they *desire* to improve student learning, not because they *feel pressured* to improve test scores or because their boss demands it. Outside pressures as a source of growth are sustainable for a time but at the cost of building morale. When people make changes because they want to or because they feel safe, their hearts and souls are into it, and therefore there will be more success than if people feel pressured into making changes.

Chapter Fifteen

Specials

Course Connections Accountability

In addition to the standard components of the reflective conversation, TBO has included special, twice-yearly teaching and learning accountability checks. Once per semester, at the observer's discretion, observers will conclude reflective conversations by having teachers show alignment between learning targets from the observed lesson and the following:

- Unit plan knowledge, skills, and understandings connected to course standards
- The summative assessment for that unit

These checks are designed to ensure alignment between the curriculum, the desired student learning, and the assessments where students demonstrate that learning. When teachers are able to show these connections to observers, there is assurance that (1) students are being taught what they are supposed to be taught and that (2) they are being assessed on the proper knowledge, skills, and understanding. When teachers consistently demonstrate alignment between standards, desired learning, and assessment, it's reasonable to presume alignment in all of the teacher's lessons. That doesn't mean that execution is ideal, only that the proper things are being taught and measured. Just doing the checks greatly increases the likelihood that teachers will make sure there is alignment.

  Checking for alignment is a straightforward, fairly quick process, usually taking around five minutes. At the conclusion of the selected conversation, let teachers know that you are hoping to do an alignment check. On occasion, teachers will ask if they can do the check another time. Accommodate teachers as long as they know the check will happen once per semester. Their reason for the request is likely that they want to refine their alignment. If they are going to do a better job of aligning between now and the next visit, then great. That's improvement.

The first step in the check is to, at the end of the conversation, ask teachers to pull up their unit plans for that course. Once they have their unit open, have them show the alignment between the learning targets and at least one facet of knowledge, skills, and/or understanding and the standard connected to it. Next, have them pull up a unit summative assessment and show the alignment there as well. Use the special columns on the observation tracking sheet to keep tabs on the progress. In the appropriate row and column, type "C" for "curriculum" and "A" for "assessment," then type "Y" or "N" as appropriate. Have teachers demonstrate alignment in two different courses/subjects during the year. To keep your schedule balanced, strive to do these checks fairly evenly over each semester so you don't overload yourself at the end of the year.

Generally, experience has shown that teachers will be able to demonstrate alignment, especially by the second year of knowing that these checks will occur. When alignment cannot be demonstrated, there are fairly common reasons for this. Teachers can be new or new to the district and are just using lessons and assessments that were handed to them without having checked for alignment. Teachers can be new to using learning targets and so haven't gotten the hang of alignment yet. New teachers often struggle to stay ahead and so haven't done the necessary work, like creating summative assessments to ensure that there is alignment. In all of these cases, developing a plan and working supportively with teachers will usually help remedy the problem. Be patient with teachers, especially in the first year of implementation or in the first year that teachers are working at that school. The yes or no isn't as important as the information it provides, which can often be used to guide future professional development decisions.

There are also more concerning reasons for the inability to demonstrate alignment, including that the school is or has been operating as a suitcase curriculum school. In this situation, it's time to bring in a curricular expert to fix the problem. Sometimes the issue is a teacher's lone-wolf mentality, which can take the form of either a teacher who is the only one teaching the course or courses or the non–team player just choosing to do his or her own thing. Either situation is an area of real concern, and it is crucial that the situation is addressed, ideally with the support and help of a curriculum coordinator and maybe even an instructional coach. Action improvement plans may be necessary.

Besides ensuring that each teacher's student learning goals are aligned with course curricula and assessments, there are other benefits to these checks. TBO is designed so that observers work their way sequentially through their observations, department by department. As such, they are generally able to see courses taught by multiple people at roughly the same time. By doing alignment checks of these courses at the same time, observers are able to easily make sure that these classes are (1) aligned in what they are teaching and (2) using common assessments. All students deserve to have courses taught to the same standards and be assessed by the same standards. These checks ensure that both of those things happen. The final benefit is that these checks help observers fulfill one area of evaluation: planning and preparation. Details on using this check for planning and preparation evaluation will be shared soon in the next part of the book.

Part 5

The Teacher Evaluation Process and Professional Development

Chapter Sixteen

Self-Assessment

Trust-Based Observation Form Rubric

Even though TBO doesn't rate or evaluate pedagogy as part of evaluation, there is still value in having a rubric that provides developmental levels of progression for teaching skills. The value lies in authentic teacher self-analysis linked to the creation of aspirational growth steps. As Charlotte Danielson, developer of *The Framework for Teaching*, told Kim Marshall (2013), "Teachers are highly motivated to improve their performance when they have themselves assessed it."

Teachers use the rubric to assess skills without fears associated with external evaluations. Absent these stressors, teachers safely use the information gleaned from their self-assessments to make informed decisions on growth priorities. They willingly use the developmental-level indicators to guide next steps, most often in the form of their action research big goal. This chapter goes over the teacher self-assessment pedagogy rubric tied to the observation form as well as the action research big goal in more detail.

TBO PEDAGOGY RUBRIC

The rubric has five levels of skill development in each pedagogical area, ranging from the most basic to the most developed. The titles of each developmental category have purposefully been framed as positively as possible to support TBO's focus on creating a safe environment conducive to risk taking. The developmental categories range from *latent* at the most basic end to *emerging*, *proficient*, *innovating*, and *leading* at the high end.

TBO has strived to make the self-assessment process as efficient and teacher friendly as possible. Teachers are asked to rate themselves twice per year, once at the beginning and again at the end of the school year. For each area on the observation form, the rubric provides descriptors for what development looks like in action at each level, from latent to leading (see table 16.1).

For each area, teachers check the box that best aligns with their current developmental level of practice. Teachers then add a narrative description for only the pedagogical skills areas tied to that year's "question of the year" and their action research big goal area for improvement. They write about their current practice and where they would like to be by the end of the year. They also create a growth goal for the big goal (addressed soon). When teachers have completed the self-assessment, they share it with their principal. Principals review it for discussion at the next reflective conversation with that teacher.

Concluding the process, at the end of the year, teachers complete the self-assessment again. The narrative this time is a reflection on growth made in the targeted goal areas.

Table 16.1.

	Latent	Emerging	Proficient	Innovating	Leading
Working Memory: 10-2 Reflection and Processing Time	Although aware of working memory, reflection is not a part of practice. At best, teacher periodically stops teaching/learning after ten minutes before moving on to a new topic.	Engages students in periodic reflections on learning that sometimes highlight critical information. The majority of students are not monitored for the desired effect of the learning.	Engages students in regular reflections on learning that highlight critical information. Monitors students for evidence of the extent to which students can recall and describe previous learning.	Adapts and creates new reflections strategies, taking into account unique student needs and situations in order for reflection to be successful in all students.	Leads and supports efforts to help other teachers advance their skills in blending brief reflection activities that build working memory into practice.

ACTION RESEARCH BIG GOAL

Closely connected to teacher self-assessment is creating an action research big goal. This goal is designed to develop or improve a specific pedagogical skill in order to improve student achievement. The most common method teachers use to determine the goal is by examining the results of the self-assessment analysis. On occasion, though, principals may dictate the goal area, especially for teachers on improvement plans.

An action research big goal is designed to develop scientist researcher mindsets. The classroom is the teacher laboratory where they experiment, and their hypothesis (action research big goal) is on the effects of using a new skill to improve student achievement. The ultimate goal is developing an embrace of risk taking and innovation as they work to improve pedagogical skills. In practice, action research big goals blend elements of traditional action research projects with an emphasis on data collection, comparative data analysis, and pieces of traditional SMART goals with particular emphasis placed on the "S" and the "M" (the "specific" and the "measurable").

The first step for teachers is choosing the skill they want to develop or improve. An example could be teachers whose self-assessment points to a latent or emerging level in cooperative learning. They choose to improve their use of cooperative learning by properly incorporating three different Kagan structures into their practice. They detail the specifics of how to use the strategies and identify how frequently they intend to use those strategies each class.

The next step is the measurable, which pulls in the action research data piece. The goal when incorporating any new skill into practice is improved student learning outcomes. There must be a comparative measurement to determine levels of success. Teachers find assessment results to compare in order to determine measurable improved student learning. These assessments compare learning results from a time before incorporating the new skill to a time after.

There are different ways to do these comparative measures. Although none are perfect, all have proven fairly solid in determining the effectiveness of the new skill on student learning outcomes. One method is to compare summative assessment results from the same unit year over year. The drawback is that the groups of students are different. Often, however, the results show stark enough differences to determine effectiveness anyway. For example, one teacher compared summative assessments year over year and saw, on average, a one-grade improvement all year, an increase so statistically significant that it holds validity even with different students.

A second method is to compare summative assessment results from new units to a prior unit the same year. The drawback here is that not all units are of equal difficulty. Again, though, often the results show stark enough differences to determine effectiveness anyway. One teacher found significant statistical improvements in the first summative results comparisons. In the next unit, though, there was only fractional improvement. When the teacher dug further, she was able to see that she had not used the new strategy as regularly during the second round. So, she made an adjustment, increased the frequency, and then saw an even greater jump the following unit.

Another method is comparing district, statewide, or national interim formative assessments, like MAP, i-Ready, or IRLA. Although growth is expected between these assessments as the year progresses, often the increased rate of growth is enough to show the effectiveness of implementing the new skill.

A final method, one that is offered reluctantly, is having a control group. When teachers teach more than one section of a class, they can use the pedagogy with one group and not another. The reluctance in offering this suggestion is the ethics of giving one group the best new efforts while withholding it from another.

With all the methods, even if growth isn't significant enough to firmly attribute it to the new strategy, the information is useful. It allows teachers and observers the opportunity to weigh what possible adjustments could be made to cause measurable improvement.

To aid teacher success in creating their goals, use a faculty meeting to explain how to craft an action research big goal. Sharing exemplars is particularly useful. Emphasize the value of risk taking and process. Many goals result in improved academic achievement, but not every goal will produce desired results, and that is okay. What matters is that teachers continue taking risks in practice; improvement will usually follow at some point.

It's also helpful to share common stumbling blocks to effective goal setting. The most common is the data comparison measure. Explaining and providing examples of effective data comparisons helps. Even with explanation, there tend to be teachers who struggle with identifying meaningful comparisons. In these instances, one-on-one meetings have helped with clarity, as has setting up a meeting between that teacher and a department peer who gets it.

Once teachers have detailed their goal and decided on their comparative measure, they will meet with their principal to discuss their goal during the next reflective conversation. Double-check their data comparison measure to make sure it works.

The differences between traditional teacher goal setting and action research big goals make a big difference in improving teaching and in student outcomes. Eliminating external pedagogy ratings reduces fear and increases teacher willingness to take risks. Data measurements comparing achievement using the strategy to achievement not using the strategy allow teachers to determine effectiveness and to make adjustments that might help. The regular conversations that observers and principals engage in on the progress of the goal keeps it constantly present in teachers' thoughts and actions, and allows them to solicit feedback. Add the focused professional development communities (discussed in chapter 19) that each teacher attends all year connected to their pedagogical growth area, and success follows.

Chapter Seventeen

Evaluation in Trust-Based Observations

Performance will always be evaluated in teaching, as it is with any job, and, like any job, it will factor into retention decisions. There is no getting around evaluation; it is part of life in the work world. What can be done in teacher evaluation, though, is eliminating an enormous obstacle to professional growth: the evaluation of pedagogy. This chapter explores TBO evaluation, what is and isn't evaluated, and why. In addition, all the steps involved in preparing for and engaging in successful summative evaluation meetings are shared.

Over the past fifty years, repeated concerns have been raised about the logic and effectiveness of combining observation for evaluation of teaching skills with observation to support professional growth. Beginning in the 1960s with clinical supervision, Goldhammer suggested that "assessing, evaluating, and judging be considered as separate from those supportive functions for which supervision is the appropriate label: coaching, helping and facilitating growth" (Goldhammer et al. 1993).

These concerns were echoed in the 1984 Rand report *Teacher Evaluation*: "Most literature questions whether a single evaluation system can handle both improvement-oriented and decision-oriented evaluation" (Wise et al. 1984), suggesting that "decision-oriented evaluations would intimidate rather than help teachers and that improvement-oriented evaluations produce data unsuited to personnel decisions" (Wise et al. 1984). Twenty years later, Stronge and Tucker (2003), authors of *Handbook on Teacher Evaluation*, acknowledged the difficulty of combining professional growth and account-ability, saying, "They are often described as mutually exclusive."

In the past decade, TNTP (2013) wrote that "nearly every teacher evalua-tion system in use today is built on the assumption that classroom observations can serve as a comprehensive teacher development tool, and a comprehensive rating tool. But recent research and experience have shown that all too often, observations accomplish neither goal." O'Leary (2017) addressed the issue too, noting that "not only were graded observations failing to assure and improve teaching quality, but the reductive and punitive ways in which observations were often used was responsible for a catalogue of detrimental effects that were impeding improvements in teacher learning."

Finally, a recent Rand report addressed reasons that the Gates Foundation's $200 million project to improve teaching quality and student achievement outcomes through the development of a more robust teacher evaluation system failed: "One reason the initiative was unsuccessful is because of the recurring issue of the difficulty in navigating the underlying tension between using evaluation for professional improvement and using it for high-stakes decisions. They had hoped that their teacher evaluation measures could be used for both purposes, but that the two goals often conflicted" (Stecher et al. 2018).

Despite these repeated warnings on the difficulty or even the possibility of effectively combining two tasks seemingly at odds with each other, no meaningful solutions on ways to resolve this issue have been made. In fact, the more common response has been to suggest that for teacher evaluation to be most beneficial, a concerted effort must be made to establish a logical link between the two purposes (Stronge and Tucker 2003). In other words, even though they don't work, find a way to make them work. Over the past few decades, that's exactly what models of observation have done: combine incongruous methods together, unsuccessfully.

The intent is worthy: combine them because evaluation is important, and obviously everyone wants to help teachers improve. But it's not working. As O'Leary (2017) writes, "The problem is that the intent and the perception do not and never will align." No matter whether they're called ratings, developmental scales, or evaluations, teachers will forever feel like they are being graded, leading to negative associations (O'Leary 2017). Instead, if educators want to make a real, sustainable difference in improving the quality of teaching through the lens of observation, then supporting rather than sorting teachers is where energies need to be focused (O'Leary 2017).

To improve the quality of teaching, and to improve student achievement, TBO rids itself of the problem by eliminating the point of interference: evaluation of pedagogy. TBO evaluates traditional indicators of workplace success for any job: planning and preparation, collegiality and communication, and professionalism. In addition, TBO removes the evaluation of pedagogy and replaces it with the evaluation of mindset.

TBO evaluates mindsets because the right mindset leads to improvement. Growth mind-sets provide people with a clear focus, all-out effort, and a bottomless trunk full of strategies; it helps their abilities grow and bear fruit

(Dweck 2006). Compare that to the fixed mindset, which stands in the way of development and change, limits achievement, and leads to inferior learning strategies. In evaluating mindsets, schools are sending a message of belief in teachers, belief in change, and belief that abilities can be cultivated. The growth mindset is the starting point for change. Evaluating mind-sets is especially exciting when people realizes that just learning about the growth mindset can cause a big shift in the way they think about themselves and their lives (Dweck 2006).

TBO EVALUATION

TBO, compared to other models, has other evaluation similarities and differences. Although using a rubric rating scale is the same, the TBO rubric is the same five-level scale used in the pedagogical self-evaluation—*latent, emerging, proficient, innovating,* and *leading*—as opposed to the more common, less positively framed four-level scale used in other models.

In the TBO rubric, *proficient* or above is considered acceptable for experienced teachers. For younger teachers, not dissimilar to other models, *emerging* is satisfactory. The number of years of experience where *emerging* is okay is to be determined by each district. Each district also has to make decisions on the basis of what is acceptable for *latent.* It is common for *latent* to be acceptable for only first- or second-year teachers in a small number of areas while they are building their overall skill base. For example, many new teachers don't do much formative assessment or differentiation when they are just starting out.

PREPARING FOR THE SUMMATIVE EVALUATION MEETING

Summative evaluation's top goal is propelling continued teaching growth while maintaining strong relationships. As such, the process, like much of TBO, is designed to support teacher actions that lead to improved student achievement. The first step is creating a feel as close as possible to that of a reflective conversation. Everyone knows that evaluative marks are given at this meeting, which increases the stakes, but that doesn't mean that the format and tone have to be different. Principals still take steps, like in any other reflective conversation, to make the meeting about strengths and about growth and to make it as positive as possible.

Being well prepared helps immensely, which takes time and work. When preparing, though, remember that using administrative assistants is one of the biggest keys to managing TBO. When you use their energies to organize and prepare, your workload is greatly reduced. Numerous preparation steps focus the meeting on the positive, create a collaborative feel, and, crucially, provide observers with information that gives a heads-up on any potential conflict areas that might arise during the discussion of domain ratings.

Teacher Self-Assessment

To provide principals with insight into teacher perceptions, teachers are sent a summative evaluation template that they use to self-rate and return prior to the meeting. Besides rating themselves, they also provide narratives on (1) their action research big goal, (2) innovation and risk taking, and (3) meaningful, special learning moments. Having this self-assessment provides valuable information, especially if there is a discrepancy between teacher and observer ratings. Knowing such differences helps immensely in preparing for the meeting. When there is agreement on the rating or if teachers rate themselves lower than the observer (which happens more often than one would think), observers go into the meeting knowing there are no worries. When an observer knows that teachers rate themselves higher in a domain than the observer, there is time to prepare. Details are discussed in the next chapter.

Principals review the end-of-year summative self-assessments to check for differences in ratings but also to clarify what teachers feel their strengths are, where their growth was, and what they'd like to improve next. Use this information to highlight agreed-on areas of strength, growth, and risk taking in the meeting. Add evidence by reviewing all the completed observation forms for each teacher and pasting relevant notes into appropriate areas of the summative evaluation form. Principals will have seen their teachers enough to write fairly accurate notes from memory, but the review tightens everything up and adds specific details (e.g., for meaningful teacher–student interaction) that might have otherwise been forgotten.

A bonus of the increased frequency of observations and reflective conversations in TBO is that it greatly eases the process of gathering evidence for this end-of-year evaluation; there are so many more observations to pull notes from. Gathering evidence ends up being a fairly speedy "copy and paste" job. Also, because all assistant principals observe as well and it's a shared document, everyone contributes evidence. By splitting the duties on who takes the preparation work lead for each teacher, the overall workload can be eased significantly.

The next preparation step is using the descriptors to assign developmental ratings. There are additional tools besides a year's worth of visits to aid observers in determining ratings. One is the opinions of other observers. Meeting with all the observers to discuss teachers and make collaborative ratings decisions is very helpful. Most of the time, agreement proves easy, but having input from everyone and consensus building when there is discrepancy helps ensure that the most accurate rating is given. Also, in conversations where teachers have a different self-rating than the principal, that consensus has been built with other observers helps immensely.

There are also factors, actions, and experiences specific to each domain that aid observers in determining ratings.

Planning and Preparation

One expectation built into the TBO system almost ensures *proficient* in planning and preparation. The checks for alignment between learning targets, curricular unit goals, and summative assessments prove a powerful motivator for teachers to plan and prepare. These unannounced checks set a high minimum expectation for planning and preparation, which generally ensures that teachers do the work and are prepared on a daily basis, resulting in almost all teachers being *proficient*.

Visual observations during visits also help. Looking at learning targets, conducting student interviews, and general observations of teaching and learning often combine to provide insight into the level of planning and preparation that has taken place. Another look-for is evidence of planning and preparation to eliminate issues of bias and equity related to areas like English-language learning, special education, and student grouping. Another source of insight on planning and preparation ratings is observation of departmental, grade-level, or course planning meetings.

Communication and Collegiality: Additional factors to consider when assigning a rating include watching teachers communicating with students both in class and out of class. Observing teachers during parent–teacher conferences is another. Another, which must be taken with a grain of salt, is feedback from parents. Feedback from peers is a legitimate consideration. Observations of teachers in communal settings, be they small- or large-group meetings or something else, provide opportunities to witness their communication and collegiality. Electronic communications, either to you directly or that you are CC'd on, provide more information as well.

Some of these communication and collegiality factors require further investigation before making final determinations on ratings because the feedback can be inaccurate. Disgruntled parents, peers, or students sometimes say things that are not true. For observers, the ability to ascertain whether information is true matters. Is something an isolated incident, a pattern, or just bad information? Be sure before making a potentially relationship-destroying incorrect rating.

Professionalism: Additional factors to consider when assigning this rating include timeliness, whether that be related to communication or making sure teachers take care of grading, providing feedback, and maintaining their records in a timely manner. Gradebooks and administrative assistants provide helpful information on professionalism related to record keeping. Another consideration involves engagement with mentoring, either giving or receiving. The issue of respecting and maintaining confidentiality falls under professionalism, too. Fulfilling responsibilities (e.g., attending mandatory meetings) and assigned supervision duties are factors. Personal integrity and following rules and regulations factor in as well.

Mindset

Two actions built into the TBO system almost ensure *proficient*. One is the action research big goal. Having an expectation for teachers to set a goal that mandates risk taking as they incorporate a new or improved pedagogical skill into their practice develops proficiency. The other action is an observer's suggestion for growth during reflective conversations. As long as teachers accept the offer of growth and work on developing an implementation plan with their observer, they demonstrate proficiency.

Other considerations factor into pushing a mindset rating decision up or down. Resistance to professional development growth is one. Examples include a regular refusal to listen to suggestions, a regular desire to sidestep growth by wanting to work on an improvement area that is not high priority, and regularly blaming the lack of student growth on outside sources. On the other end of the mindset spectrum, unsolicited teacher actions or inquiries on ways to improve the school, their students, or themselves professionally certainly push teachers toward *innovative* or *leading*.

Ratings Discrepancies and Low Ratings

It is challenging to determine the best course of action to take when teachers are below *proficient* in any domain and/or if their rating is below yours. Start by weighing different factors in each situation with each teacher. Use your time spent with teachers and the input from other observers to make your best prediction of their reactions to less-than-good news. In other words, what is your perception of their mindset during challenging times that requires timely action toward improvement?

A factor often helpful in determining likely teacher reaction is their years of teaching experience. With younger teachers, a latent or emerging rating will be less surprising to them: they are newer, after all. With newer teachers, the opportunity to talk about and develop a plan for improvement in a way that will most likely be perceived positively by both parties is greater. With more experienced teachers, sharing a lower rating, depending on the teacher, runs the risk of leading to a more complicated and difficult discussion. Use all of the information and your emotional intelligence to make decisions on how to proceed in the meeting. More information on engaging in difficult conversations is shared in the next chapter.

THE MEETING

Now that you are prepared, the meeting begins just like in the reflective conversation, in their room, sitting beside teachers, and asking questions. Unless you are the sole principal in your building, having an assistant in the meetings is valuable for many reasons. They might have a better relationship with that teacher and be the best one to lead the meeting, and there is a witness just in case.

The summative evaluation form guides you. Begin by asking teachers to provide an oral narrative of their year. Teachers are encouraged to focus on their growth, their action research big goal, examples of risk taking, and any particularly special or meaningful learning moments and desired next steps in learning. Beginning with questions allows observers to once again show immediate interest by listening. As in reflective conversations, observers type notes while the teacher is sharing. Remembering the action research big goal is discussed regularly; sharing how the goal went is really a review.

Observers continue by asking more questions. Ask teachers to share their ratings and reasoning: they are welcome to orally share examples of supporting evidence for each of the domains. Once again, observers listen and type notes where appropriate.

Next, observers, like in the reflective conversation, share observed strengths and growth—but for the whole year, not a single visit. These noticed strengths can range from pedagogical, to any area related to the four domains, to specific examples of teacher risk taking or innovation, to any other growth area that was noticed over the course of the school year.

Principals then share their domain ratings and evidence with teachers, which is a straightforward process when there are no discrepancies. When sharing the ratings when there are discrepancies, share the ratings in order; don't skip the one with a discrepancy. If you skip it, both sides will know there is a negative rating coming, and that alone will interfere with the rest of the discussion.

When there is a discrepancy, begin by sharing your rating, acknowledging the difference, and then seek clarity from teachers on their rating. Even though teachers may have provided evidence earlier, inquire further as to why they gave themselves that rating. Ask them if they would like to share more examples that support their rating. Remember, even in TBO, observers spend only a tiny fraction of the teacher's work life with them. You can easily be unaware of multiple examples of higher-level action that occurred over the course of the year, and, presented with new information, it could very well make sense to change your rating.

Asking for details and listening helps even when, in the end, there is no agreement and the observer rates teachers lower than teachers think they deserve. Teachers often feel better just because their boss took the time to listen to them.

When further observer questioning does not lead to a rating change and/or there is any rating below proficient, your preparation will help. At this point, preparation provides you with a good idea of the best course of action to take. Where the anticipation is that teachers will be okay with a lower rating or a discrepancy and they will be receptive to a growth opportunity, even in the form of an action improvement plan, you can comfortably proceed. When the anticipation is that teachers' sense of vulnerability will kick in so that the reaction will be less than open and positive, the realm of difficult conversations is about to be entered. The how-to's on those conversations is discussed in the next chapter along with action improvement plans.

For either anticipated response, the discussion of the improvement plan has to take place before the end of the year so that summer professional development support opportunities can be taken advantage of by teachers. The best course of action at this point is to ask teachers if they would like to talk about improvement steps now or later. This choice respects teachers by providing them with the opportunity to pick the time and space, both physical and emotional, that works best for them to engage in a difficult conversation.

Chapter Eighteen

Action Improvement Plans and Difficult Conversations

As teachers begin their careers, their newness usually shows, and over their first years, with practice and support, they progress and improve fairly quickly. So, not surprisingly, experience is a big factor in teaching quality; so is talent, care for kids, and a desire to make a difference. Besides these factors, the root obstacle to higher-quality teaching is almost always tied to one of the evaluative domains.

Poor planning and preparation result in weak lessons, low engagement, and often chaos because teaching activities are not ordered or organized. Poor communication and collegiality cause relationship or clarity problems that interfere with the ability to help students thrive. Concerns in this area also frequently cause problems between the teacher and parents and peers, problems that interfere with school culture. Fixed mindsets prevent risk taking, interfere with growth efforts, and prevent improved teaching. Poor professionalism impacts school morale, and when teachers aren't on top of things like grading (and hence feedback), a student's ability to improve is limited.

Lower development in any of the evaluative domains is cause for concern. When issues in any of them are noticed, worked on in a supported manner, yet persist, they must be addressed in order to help teachers, to improve school culture, and, most important, to help students. The logical path forward when previous efforts have proven unfruitful is through a formal action improvement plan specifically designed to support growth in the targeted area. The plans and the conversations, where they are discussed, can be difficult and are the focus of this chapter.

Before digging fully into action improvement plans and difficult conversations, it's important for observers to consider some additional factors of teaching and schools. First, no school will ever be made up of only excellent or even the top 25 percent of teachers, and that's okay. The goal is the same: support the development of improved teaching from wherever each teacher currently is. To get all teachers innovating or leading is a fantastic aspiration, but not everyone will reach that goal in their pedagogy or in the evaluative domains.

The second consideration is the reason that having teachers with a variety of skill levels is fine. Some teachers who aren't innovating or leading in teaching make up for it in other ways. There are many teachers ranging from so-so to very good who bring intangibles to the table that factor prominently into the success of a school. These intangibles raise the value of a really good, a good, or even an average or so-so teacher a notch or two. More important, schools wouldn't function nearly as successfully without these intangibles. Embrace these teachers; value their whole package, not just their pedagogy.

Teachers possessing intangibles are often the ones students feel comfortable talking to about their problems, the ones who make them laugh and support them when they cry. They are the ones involved in activities that go above and beyond the call of duty. Examples include providing extra support, be that academic or social-emotional, for students outside of class hours, leading groups or clubs, coaching, running service projects, and chaperoning. These teachers put in extra time all year; they ask you what you need. These teachers help schools thrive.

ACTION IMPROVEMENT PLANS

Ratings decisions that lead to an action improvement plan are usually easy to make. *Latent* preparation and planning is obvious during reflective conversation accountability checks and organization issues that clearly affect the class. Latent professionalism is clear because it is easy to spot when basic everyday responsibilities are not being handled. Latent communication and collegiality is easy to spot during classroom interactions and via complaints received that affect morale. The latent fixed mindset is easily identified by a near-constant resistance to change. Identifying the low ratings is easy; the problem is that your past efforts to support improvement have been unsuccessful, hence the need for an action improvement plan.

Despite knowing that a teacher requires an improvement plan, some principals struggle with following through, and usually it's because of a desire to be liked. In Glasser's (1998) *Choice Theory*, they would be the ones driven most powerfully by a love and belonging need. It's understandable; everyone wants to be liked. It's natural for anyone to worry that when the plan is broached, the teacher will be upset and not like you and tell others, resulting in widespread feelings of resentment because you "targeted" a teacher. In most instances, the worry doesn't align with real action. The truth is that other teachers are keenly aware of who the struggling teachers are and actually appreciate that you are taking action. Ironically, in taking action, you end up being more respected. So, no matter your worries, take action because not doing so can damage a school's culture. Take action because doing so is what's best for kids.

As you prepare, having a growth mindset lays the foundation for success. Create the plan assuming best intentions and with the absolute conviction that teachers will make growth such that you will both look back on the plan later, thinking, "Wow, what an improvement!"

At the same time, even with a positive mindset toward the outcome, not all action plans will lead to success. Truth be told, you can probably predict which teachers are not likely to achieve the desired improvements. Despite this fact, do everything possible to support the teacher and believe that the teacher will do everything possible to achieve the necessary growth. Why? First, it's the right thing to do, and you want to model the mindset that you expect your teachers to use with students. Second, if success is not achieved, it is much better that there be no question about the motivations or efforts to support the teacher if dismissal actions become the next step. Driven by what is best for students, the last thing a principal wants is for the process to be delayed because motive or lack of support is questioned.

When developing the plan, whether you use the TBO or a district template, the goal is the same: for the teacher to make sufficient progress so that the plan is no longer necessary. Do the following to properly prepare when creating the plan:

- Consult with other observers to seek their input. Together, you create the best plan.
- To signal success, experienced teachers must reach *proficient*. For less experienced teachers, they must attain at least *emerging*. So, use specific language detailing desired growth outcomes and specify what successful action looks like; template descriptors help.
- Offer avenues for support. The support can include any combination of mentoring from peers, coaches, an assistant principal, or you; books or links to articles targeting the growth area; or professional development courses or training. Do your homework.
- Have someone review the document to ensure that there are no issues of bias in the plan.
- Include monitoring, time-line, and deadline details. Usually, observers must adhere to district-mandated time lines, so record these dates.
- Include potential consequences, even dismissal. Observers don't want to minimize the seriousness of an action improvement plan.

DIFFICULT CONVERSATIONS

Whether or not an action improvement plan meeting turns into a difficult conversation, the goal is to make the best out of a potentially tough situation by being as positive, hopeful, and gentle as possible while dealing with a negative situation. You address and confront issues with the goal of transforming the area of growth into a strength, creating a brightly transformed future.

Success is the goal, but it's not fun to think about let alone engage in a conversation with someone who is being told that something related to their work is not up to snuff. It's unsettling. In discussing these conversations, know that some won't be difficult and know that the difficult ones won't suddenly become easy because of some magic panacea. However, in addressing difficult conversations, you will increase the likelihood for success as you learn about the following:

- Normal brain responses to potentially difficult encounters and powering through fight-or-flight inclinations, thus making the choice to engage in the conversations easier
- Preparation tips, which often increase the likelihood that the meetings lead to growth

Difficult conversations are most likely to occur during reflective conversations that include suggestions, action improvement plan meetings, or notice of dismissal meetings. In each case, there is time between when you know the conversation is necessary and when the meeting takes place, which is a blessing because it allows you to prepare mentally and physically.

These conversations are frightening for teachers and for principals. As a principal, it's important to acknowledge your fears because navigating them is the most challenging yet vital step in managing these talks. As soon as you realize that a potentially difficult conversation is looming, you are likely to experience unsettling feelings of fear and anxiety. These feelings are from the brain's limbic system working to protect you. Your amygdala is creating a fight-or-flight response in reaction to what the meeting could potentially become, namely, an ugly conflict.

This sensation is the brain anticipating something negative, like saying something that is met with a harsh negative response by the teacher. The result is your mind being flooded with all the worst possible scenarios as the likely occurrence. Your brain is preparing you to either fight or flee; it is normal.

The challenge is understanding what your brain is doing and then not letting it rule your actions and prevent you from engaging in the conversation. The likelihood of the outcome manifesting itself as the negative messages your brain is sending you is incredibly small. The one way to discover that the meeting won't be as bad as you think is by forcing yourself to have the meeting despite your brain's warnings. When you do, it is an amazing relief to realize that things turned out just fine.

My first meaningful experience with this phenomenon was in a previous career as a basketball coach. Reliable sources told me that they had overheard my assistant coach bad-mouthing me to players. The assistant coach was a holdover from the previous staff, and maybe that contributed to his actions. No matter the reason, this situation required dismissal. On learning the story, my amygdala did just what it was supposed to do. Every potential negative outcome from confronting him, screaming, yelling, throwing things, you name it, ran through my head, over and over. The result: paralyzed by fear, I took no action.

Finally, a more veteran coach told me that I had to get rid of him, plain and simple. So, reluctantly, I set up a meeting. When he came in, after exchanging pleasantries, I told him I thought it would be best that I go in a different direction with a new assistant. Before I even had a chance to explain why, he stood up, shook my hand, said he understood, thanked me for the opportunity, and walked out.

I was shocked, but what a revelation. Since then, whenever I have to engage in a difficult conversation, the same fears and anxieties surface every time, even though I know my thoughts are not the likely outcome. However, forcing myself to take action that first time has made it so much easier to take action ever since.

So, the first step is preparing to overcome your own mind by recognizing that the mind's first fearful scenarios are not the likely outcome. The more often you engage in these potentially difficult conversations, the easier it is to experientially know it's the mind trying to protect you; the chances of a bad conversation are slim. That's not to say that there won't be a difficult conversation (on rare occasions there will be), but further preparation minimizes the chances.

These brain messages do hold power; honor the reasons they occur and prepare to make the *fight* a peaceful one. Prepare for the possibility of the meeting going bad. This preparation often makes the difference when teacher reactions can lead to a potentially difficult conversation. Your preparation can turn bad into good (or at least neutral).

Preparation

- Enlist the help of your assistant principals ahead of the meeting. Their insight into particular teachers and, for that matter, their relationship might be better than yours. Their ability to gauge teachers and their potential reactions might make the difference between success and failure. In addition to enlisting their insight, invite them to join you and/or even lead the meeting if it's agreed that it will help. Also, having an additional person in the meeting provides a witness, which is good for all parties.

- Enlist the help of peer principals or mentors. Besides asking for their advice, ask them to challenge you on what some of your own potential stumbling blocks to success with this teacher might be. You might be harboring bias of some sort for legitimate or illegitimate reasons. As Brown (2012) writes, you have to be willing to ask for and receive feedback in order to be good at giving it. The truth is that sometimes the size, severity, or complexity of a problem doesn't always reflect the emotional reactivity to it. A peer can help observers get to the same side of the table as the teacher so that they can be present and therefore be much more likely to see the change that's requested.
- Anticipate the possible or likely negative responses teachers will provide to questions or issues that will be brought up in the meeting. Use these potential responses to determine ahead of time how you will respond to their response.

The following story shows what can happen when you have not prepared for an unexpected teacher response.

I discovered that a specialist teacher was not pushing into some of her classes. I then learned the crazy details during a reflective conversation with her officemate, who was talking about the difficulty of pushing into her classes while also getting her prep work done. So I asked if other specialists were struggling as well. The pained expression on her face told me everything.

This teacher, whose moral code is beyond reproach, proceeded to tell me about a conversation she and the teacher in question had recently had. She expressed frustration on how hard it was to push into all of her classes. The other teacher responded by saying that the schedule was only a guideline for push-ins and she didn't have to go to all of those classes. The teacher I was speaking with explained that she couldn't not push in. The teacher in question responded by saying, "Oh, you mean morals. No, it's okay."

So, I dropped into the teacher's office after school to talk about this issue. I sat down and expressed concern about her not pushing into classes. She said she pushed into all of her classes. I told her I walked into multiple classes she was supposed to be in and she wasn't there. She said I must not have been there the whole time because she was there for part of the classes.

Not prepared for these denials, what was my response? My voice raised in anger as I told her I knew that wasn't true. I couldn't tell her about the other conversation; they were friends, and the other teacher begged me not to. The meeting ended with my being angry and her being defensive.

I scheduled another meeting, deciding that as long as she admitted, for any reason, that she had missed a push-in just once, I would work with her. She was a decent teacher and offered *intangibles*. In an astounding meeting, I kept offering conceivable reasons that she might have missed class: her student council duties, she forgot one time, she wasn't feeling well. I told her these things happen on occasion; it's okay. She insisted she never missed a push-in. Working in the world of annual contracts, I made the decision to not renew someone who could not be honest.

It was surreal, but it was over, or so I thought. Late in the year, human resources approached me about a grievance regarding the way I treated her in the first meeting, all because I hadn't prepared for her answer. The grievance ended up being denied, but I learned a valuable lesson. If I had prepared for a negative response, I would have avoided raising my voice in anger when she lied. The result would have been a much less contentious meeting and maybe even a different ending.

- Role-play the meeting if you are particularly worried about how it might go. Use one of your assistants and practice calm responses to their responses.
- Prepare to postpone the meeting. Tell yourself ahead of time that if things aren't going well, for whatever reason, you have permission to reschedule the meeting for a later date in order to better prepare or to let emotions calm down.
- If the meeting ends up being rescheduled, another option is to be prepared to ask teachers if they would like to bring someone into the meeting with them. Doing so demonstrates respect for teachers and hopefully adds to their comfort level.

The Meeting

- Allow yourself to be vulnerable. Valuing your own vulnerability is not a weakness: it's courage beyond measure (Brown 2012). Admit your fears. You can say something like, "I'm feeling frightened to be bringing up this issue." Some people feel they could never tell another person that they were frightened for fear that they would be picked to pieces. When you choose to state your feelings along with the reasons for wanting teachers to change, you are likely to notice how differently they respond. Doing so will help you realize and appreciate the potential impact of expressing vulnerability (Rosenberg 2015).
- Be gentle and use empathy. Listening is important; when people are upset, they often need empathy before they can hear what is being said to them. Defuse stress by empathizing with others (Rosenberg 2015).

- When teachers express resistance, the root is often some negative past experience that caused a retreat into complacency, a lack of grit, or a fixed mindset. It's common to hear an argument that what they are doing works. Perhaps, but education is a constantly changing craft, with regular developments on more effective ways to foster and support learning. With these researched, improved practices must come efforts to embrace—or at least attempt—new strategies, and this requires risk taking. What they are doing may work, but in trying something new, teachers are likely to discover something that works better.

When you encounter this resistance, the question is, how do you respond? Inquire. Inquire about a time in their life when they have overcome an obstacle. Discussing a time when they have turned obstruction into success has the power to lead teachers toward embracing or reembracing a risk-taking, growth mindset. Inquire about the reasons they are resisting change efforts. There are fixed mindset triggers, and sometimes inquiry can help teachers identify and work with these triggers (Dweck 2016). The hope is that they unlock and work through their triggers on the path to risk taking.

When people resist, they don't have to stay in a fixed mindset. People can be put into a growth mindset by telling them that an ability can be learned and that this task will give them a chance to do that. Have them read a scientific article that teaches them the growth mindset, an article that describes people who did not have natural ability but who developed exceptional skills (Dweck 2006).

- Ask teachers their thoughts on the best way to achieve the goals. What do they believe will help them the most? Make the process as collaborative as possible; all the previous work on building trusting relationships with each teacher helps now. Even though you have a plan to support the growth, be prepared to adjust it to fit the desires of the teacher. Find the blend that fits best for both parties.
- Encouragement helps, so reassure teachers that risk taking and failure are embraced. Let them know that as long as there is a genuine effort, including an effort to learn from failures, things ought to be okay. It's not always okay, but often it is.
- A candid expression of concern regarding the seriousness of the situation can help. If teachers don't seem to be getting it, then laying out your worries can shake some people into a sense of urgency. Read people and determine whom this might help. Your own feelings of desperation and frustration are a sign that it is time to share. In this vulnerable time, it has worked well when sharing potential consequences to also share that you hope that the plan will be successful, but you have to share the worst, too.

In the end, these plans and the conversations that follow are impossible to predict with certainty. The best you can do is prepare well, use the tips that seem most appropriate to the moment, and work to be as empathetic and understanding as you can while responding the best that you can in the moment when working with your teachers in this fragile situation.

Dismissal Decisions

Ultimately, what teachers decide to do with the plan and support is up to them. Like in any profession, a small percentage will resist or be unable to make sufficient progress. That's when a change is necessary. Using TBO, the mechanisms are in place, even without evaluating pedagogy, to support dismissal when required.

Sometimes, by asking the right questions regarding that person's success narrative, their life goals, and reasoning for doing their work, teachers can be counseled to their own discovery of a better alternative career path. That will not always be the case; sometimes dismissal will be contentious and can end in hard feelings from teachers. Part of a principal's job, though, is doing what's best for students, which means difficult decisions and difficult conversations.

Chapter Nineteen

TBO and Professional Development

A commitment to professional learning is important, not because teaching is of poor quality and must be fixed, rather because teaching is so difficult that we can always improve it.—Charlotte Danielson

Teachers deserve professional development (PD) that is flexible and responsive to teacher variance yet firmly committed to teacher growth. Unfortunately, to many educators, "high-quality staff development" is an oxymoron. The list of complaints about workshops is long: "drive-by" workshops, one-size-fits-all presentations, "been there, done that" topics, little or no modeling of what is being taught, and a lack of follow-up (Strickland 2009). In order for observations to maximize teaching growth, the system has to be comprehensive, which means that PD has to be part of the process. TBO integrates PD into the system in ways that provide the meaningful learning that teachers deserve. This chapter explores the PD that is part of TBO, PD that is relevant for teachers and that positively impacts student learning.

One way of connecting PD to observations is through what most of this book has been about: frequent observations, reflective conversations, and the suggestions and support that accompany the process. Research backs the effectiveness of this method: when principals engage in periodic, short, focused, individual conversations with teachers, they advance professional learning and produce positive change in teacher behavior (Moss and Brookhart 2009). This method achieves O'Leary's (2017) suggestion that the goal of observation is to "make lesson observation the most valuable opportunity for one-to-one personalized PD to develop the skills of the teacher."

TBO incorporates PD into the system in two other ways. The first is through the "question of the year" and the schoolwide PD connected to it. The second is through a combination of action research big goals, "Evidence

of" categories, and the introduction of professional development communities (PDCs).

QUESTION-OF-THE-YEAR PD

The connection between PD and the question of the year is a natural one. As
discussed previously, the question is designed to target and support schoolwide improvement for one year on an area where a large percentage of the
teachers have room for growth. Support is provided by asking each teacher
the question and engaging in talks surrounding the progress and development
of this skill during every reflective conversation. Support is also provided in
the form of consistent, relevant PD training all year.

To begin this PD, create regular blocks of time for it. Assuming that your
school is like most, where there is one morning or afternoon period of time
per week dedicated to meetings, devote at least one week per month to
question-of-the-year PD. The next step is deciding on the growth area. For
planning purposes, make the decision no later than spring in the year prior to
beginning. Use observations and your leadership team to determine the area.
Based on your teachers' most pressing growth areas, choose the one that you,
as leaders, believe will have the highest impact on improved student learning
outcomes. Once decided, create the question. A single question (or a series of
two or three connected questions) is fine.

Now it's time to decide who's going to lead the PD. The best place to
start is with your in-house experts, your own teachers. A huge benefit of the
frequent visits is that you know who is strongest at different areas of teaching. Engage these experts in discussions on coleading PD for this pedagogical area. The best part is that by tapping into these teachers' strengths, you
are empowering them and developing teacher leaders. You also provide the
added benefit of having active practitioners fill at least some of the facilitator
roles. Although there is immense value in active practitioners, if the principal
or one of the assistants has particular strengths in the target area, use them as
well. Combining everyone's strengths leads to the best PD.

Once you have engaged the commitment of the targeted teacher leaders,
it's time to begin planning the training. As an aside, if you can obtain stipend
funds for these teacher leaders, do it. Teachers aren't always driven by money, but it adds incentive to say yes to leading training, and it's a fantastic way
to say thanks. As you plan, important considerations and steps that aid in
discussing and preparing for the training include the following:

- The current developmental levels of teachers in the target area. Use teachers' own self-assessment ratings to determine the range and frequency of
  where teachers are. Realize that some teachers might have misassessed

themselves, in which case leadership judgments can be used to reposition these teachers. This information helps in knowing where to start and what areas to differentiate, determining subleaders, and creating groups for small-team, cooperative training activities.

- Determining leaders' particular areas of expertise. This information helps you know who is best suited to lead what and in making decisions on additional training that leaders might require. Planning early allows time to register people for summer workshops.
- Developing plans for the PD sessions. Require that all training be practical, can be demonstrated, and is actionable and includes practice time.
- Make determinations on whether teacher unit plans will require adjustments because of the new learning. Include time for that work if it is deemed necessary. Providing teachers with time to do this work plays a huge role in building teacher buy-in and support.
- Troubleshoot; think ahead. Anticipate potential stumbling blocks, particularly with challenging personnel, and develop responses ahead of time.

Some have asked a fair question: Does question-of-the-year PD have value for all teachers? Remember that the chosen area is one in which a majority (often a great majority) of teachers have room to grow. Also, there is no limit to the number of facilitators you can use. So, for teachers skilled enough, even with differences in ability levels, there is room for constructive use of all in-house experts to lead or support to some degree. Finally, since teaching others is the highest form of learning, these teachers receive the added benefit of becoming even more expert at the pedagogical focus area. So, all teachers do benefit.

PDC AND ACTION RESEARCH BIG GOALS

PDCs are minicommunities of teachers within a building who meet regularly to train in, discuss, celebrate the success of, and troubleshoot concerns related to implementation of a chosen area of pedagogical growth. The pedagogy that teachers choose for their PDC is one of the "Evidence of" categories on the observation form and is tied to their action research big goal.

The term PDC is used to distinguish itself from professional learning communities (PLCs). PLCs originally had multiple purposes, including data analysis of student assessment results and pedagogical small-group learning. Over time, though, PLCs morphed more exclusively into being the DuFour model of student data analysis, which no doubt has great value. PDC provides a specific definition for groups of teachers who consistently and regularly work together in a safe environment over the course of a school year to improve, support one another, and grow their skills in specific chosen areas of pedagogy. The end goal of a PDC is improved student learning outcomes through more proficient teaching in the chosen area.

PDCs are a more effective method for incorporating PD into a school. First, connecting PD to the model's areas of pedagogy is more practical and useful for teachers. Teacher buy-in is greater because teachers are provided significant decision-making autonomy in choosing an area for growth. Finally, the breadth of different areas to study allows PDCs to fit the strength and growth needs of all faculty members.

PDCs carve out time for teachers to try out new ways of teaching while removing the censure of potential failure. The goal is for teachers to have explicit permission to innovate and experiment in a culture of learning together so that learning about what not to do is valued as highly as learning what to do (O'Leary 2017). PDCs allow teachers to grow in practice by receiving the guidance and support—the cumulative and collective wisdom about teaching—that a community of collegial discourse provides (Palmer 2017).

In many ways, PDCs function in a manner similar to question-of-the-year PD. Observers ask questions and engage in reflective discussions with each teacher on the progress of their action research big goal. There is a commitment to the same regular and consistent pattern of one learning block of time per month for the PDCs to meet. Because you know who is best at what, you engage the cooperation of teacher leaders to facilitate the learning sessions. The strengths of principals or assistant principals as facilitators are again tapped if there is a match. You determine if additional training will help the success of these facilitator leaders in the year ahead. You plan or, more likely, oversee the planning of the teacher leaders since there are so many areas of pedagogy in which to make plans. This work is done well ahead of time because facilitators know they are leading a PDC in the spring before meetings begin. Determinations are made on setting aside time to tweak unit plans, and time is spent thinking about troubleshooting areas. Other similarities, elements, and considerations for question of the year and PDC include the following:

- Finding and using more than one teacher leader for each group is fine if there are enough personnel to warrant it. If some have more than one and others don't, that is okay.
- For question of the year, the area of pedagogy changes every year, so there are different leader/facilitators each year. For PDCs, there are also different facilitators each year. In the second year and beyond, principals, with the help of current leaders, determine from among each PDC group's current members whom to recruit to lead the following year.
- For both, each session after the first includes not only new learning and content but also opportunities for teachers to share, discuss, and support

one another through successes and struggles in a safe environment where everyone learns from everyone.

- For both, pre-assessments are done, allowing teachers to share where they are in their development and, more important, to share what they hope to gain from the year of PD.
- For both, participants develop their learning goals by using the TBO self-assessment rubric developmental levels. Individual goals for teachers will vary depending on their current level of proficiency. Some teachers will aim to go from latent to proficient, while others may aim for leading. A goal might be to develop where they lead that particular PDC the next year. All goal choices are okay as long as they improve teaching.

There are also differences in the way the question of the year and PDCs function. In PDCs, there are eight areas to choose from, one for each pedagogical area that isn't the one used for the question of the year. For example, if question-of-the-year PD was formative assessment, then teachers would choose their PDC from among learning targets, relationships, management, cooperative learning, working memory, questioning, feedback, and differentiation. Each PDC works together in smaller teams, not as an entire faculty. Another difference is that, generally, teachers choose their PDC and connect it to their action research big goal.

There are exceptions to teachers being allowed to choose their PDC. One is for a struggling teacher, often one on an action improvement plan. Here a principal has the right to steer or direct the teacher into the PDC that is the most pressing area for improvement. Also, exceptions are made for PDC facilitators. They are not required to attend other PDCs during the year they are facilitating; they occur at the same time anyway. Not to worry, as teachers lead a PDC for only one year before handing it off to a new in-house expert. For these leaders, individual conversations are used to determine their action research big goal for the year. They might choose to become stronger in their leadership area or choose another area and do independent study learning. Either choice is fine.

MORE ON PDCS

- Principals meet with PDC leaders at the beginning of the year to establish and go over support protocols and learning goals with an eye toward differentiating for the needs of each teacher learner. Like teachers with students, it's essential that leaders understand the importance of reaching teachers where they are.
- PDC groups create shareable training/planning/learning documents, be that through Google, Atlas Rubicon, or some other method. These docu-

ments create a record of the work that helps the current group and future-year groups as well. They also allow eager learners to use them even if it isn't an area of focus that year. In the end, these documents become part of a series of schoolwide resource guides available to all faculty.

- Have at least one principal or assistant principal not lead a PDC. This school leader makes the rounds of all eight PDCs every meeting. They check in, observe the goings-on, and share back with the rest of the leadership team.
- The principal and/or assistant principals meet individually with PDC leaders between visits to check in on progress and next steps, a kind of reflective conversation.
- Each PDC team discusses where and what they want to learn and practice next; they make their own decisions. A variance on what individual members of each PDC want is not only allowed but also encouraged as part of good differentiated practice.

FURTHER PD TIPS, SUGGESTIONS, AND GUIDELINES

Finally, it's worth taking some time to look at some additional general PD tips, suggestions, and guidelines that help ensure learning success:

- Avoid new-initiative overload. The PDC and question of the year are the only targeted PD areas for the school every year. If there are too many new ideas and plans for a year, the result is that teachers become overloaded and disenchanted. Encourage teachers with manageable steps rather than trying to do too many things at once (Tomlinson 2015).
- As you add new practices, don't be afraid to eliminate previous initiatives the school has been using. Too often, leaders are reluctant to take away, thinking it won't look good to remove a previously endorsed initiative. Although the worry is understandable, teachers appreciate that you are taking something off their plate and are consciously working to not overload them.
- If it works for a grade- or subject-level team, there are advantages to having them work on the same PDC at the same time. Advantages include shared responsibility for planning and greater opportunities for feedback discussions on progress with the new work.
- Leaders must model good teaching in their PDC. Modeling good practice of their PDC is essential, but so is modeling good teaching in general, including every "evidence of" area on the observation form. Leaders will lose their audience if they aren't walking the talk.

In the end, TBO's PD methods provide avenues for social learning, a core functional element in a school-based professional community that is necessary to support more ambitious classroom instruction. The goal is for trust not only in principal work with teachers but also in teacher work with teachers to function as the social glue necessary for this work to coalesce and be maintained (Bryk and Schneider 2002). The hope is that TBO and, within it, its PD provide a means for meaningful teacher growth, for the growth of any craft depends on shared practice and honest dialogue among the people who do it. Our willingness to try and fail as individuals is severely limited when we are not supported by a community that encourages such risks. The resources we need in order to grow as teachers are abundant within the community of colleagues. Good talk about good teaching enhances professional practice (Palmer 2017).

Part 6

Bringing It All Together

Chapter Twenty

Building TBO Success

With any new endeavor, it makes sense to do everything possible to set yourself up for initial and sustained success, and that's what this final chapter is about. Thoughts and suggestions on creating implementation success are shared. Ideas are also shared on successfully blending TBO into more traditional practice when district or legislative regulations prevent full implementation of the model. There is an exploration of leadership style and the importance of potentially making personal changes in order to build teacher trust. Finally, actions that sustain and build on TBO success over time are shared.

IMPLEMENTATION

Implementation works best when steps have been taken to build teachers' interest in and acceptance of TBO. Being well prepared is the key, and there are two main areas of preparation: training yourselves and explaining the model.

First, make sure that you and your assistant principals are as well trained as possible. As soon as you know you are going to make the switch, start spending significant time familiarizing yourselves with all of the areas of the observation form, from the questions to the "Evidence of" section and its "Toolbox Possibilities." The more solidly you know the form, the more effective and confident you will be doing your observations and reflective conversations. To deepen your knowledge and confidence, as part of your preparation (assuming you have sufficient leadership personnel), teach minilessons to each other while someone observes, takes notes, and engages in mock reflective conversations. The group of you then engage in conversations about the just completed mini-observation process. Doing so allows you to work out bugs ahead of time.

The second step is preparing for the faculty meeting where you explain the change to TBO. The keys are sharing the TBO system, including how the observation form works, how evaluation works, and the benefits of switching.

The system is a straightforward explanation: a continuous cycle of short observations and reflective conversations focused on strengths and, eventually, supported risk taking to benefit teaching and learning growth. The process is not about the "out to getcha" mindset that many teachers have experienced. Share the form with teachers and explain the questions and the purpose of each; share the rationale for the "Evidence of" areas, highlighting the "Toolbox Possibilities" functionality as a growth resource tool. Focus on risk taking/innovative practice. Let teachers know that if you see them trying something new, even if it doesn't go well, they can expect nothing but support for taking chances. Explain and highlight the evaluation differences between TBO and the previous model, which ought to be easy and come as a joyous relief to teachers. This book has explained TBO's benefits clearly, and since the benefits are so much to teachers' liking, well-being, and peace of mind, this explanation will be straightforward and fun.

Providing teachers time to process the information in small groups is recommended, as is letting them ask questions. Often the best answer to questions is that, with time, teachers will feel the difference and really enjoy the new model.

There are variances in these meetings, including whether you are implementing the whole system and whether the style of leadership you practice will be new. It is a more complicated meeting if TBO is a significant style switch for the principal. Those issues will be explored next.

BLENDING

In an ideal world, schools and districts fully adopt the TBO model. As an idealist, confident that the model works best when all elements are implemented, there is also an understanding of practical reality; not all schools or districts will be willing or able to adopt the evaluation changes immediately. Cognizant of this possibility, know that the model can still achieve success even if the evaluation change cannot be made right away. If you find yourself in this situation, don't let the evaluation roadblock stand in the way of adopting the rest of TBO.

No matter the job, a leader who builds strong trusting relationships with workers will be more successful in maximizing employee production. People will do more for those they like, trust, and respect. So when compromise is required, all the trust-building actions in the model are the same, but there are also steps you might be able to take that further help the cause and build toward full adoption of TBO:

* If at all possible, eliminate rating individual lesson observation. Save this task for the end of the year. Rating each lesson will make building a sense of safety for teachers nearly impossible.
* Seek permission to pilot a few teachers in your school in the TBO evaluation method. In many traditional models, there are a few teachers every year who are not on a traditional evaluation schedule. Perhaps you can gain the cooperation of some of them to engage in the pilot.
* With time, as you build trust and teachers experience the benefits of the model, you might be able to convince teachers to petition, with the union's help, the school district to adopt the new model for the school, even if as a pilot.

CHANGE

As you have read this book, it's likely that many different thoughts and feelings have ruminated through your head and heart. Hopefully at the top of the list is adopting TBO as your new model of teacher observation. You have also probably been analyzing your own leadership, your work with observation, and the relationships and trust you may or may not have built with teachers. For some, the analysis has been encouraging. For others, feelings of anxiety about adopting TBO may have surfaced. You're intrigued but realize that, because of current observation practice and/or your own leadership actions, there is a gap between where you are and where TBO asks you to be. Fear not if this is the case; your knowledge of mindsets lets you know you can make the changes necessary to become a successful TBO practitioner.

To check where you are, it's time for a brief leadership self-analysis, the intent of which is not to be critical but rather to take an honest look at actions in order to become better principals. If you find yourself saying, "That's me" or "I've done that," it's okay.

Have you been guilty of teacher bashing? Have you had thoughts like "You have to watch 'em" or "They just don't get it"? Have you been overly critical or judgmental of your teachers? Have you made snap judgments and not been open to the possibility of teachers growing? Have you regularly been doing important, vital things that have kept you in your office most of the day? Have you been the hard-driving, type-A personality who gets things done without thinking about how teachers respond to this style? Have you seen observations as a chore? Have you delivered feedback mostly electronically because of time constraints or because you were fearful of the reflective conversation? Have you become disengaged? Has empathy for the challenges of teaching been missing? Because there are so many responsibilities, has the building of relationships been low on your priority list? Have you had good intentions but overloaded teachers with suggestions? Have you been frustrated by the lack of teaching improvement? Have you been guilty of playing favorites? Are teachers held to one narrow standard rather than acknowledged for their unique gifts and contributions? (Brown 2012).

If any of your answers are yes, you are in good company. Sometimes it's the model, sometimes it's external pressures, and sometimes it's a style choice. No matter the reason, change is possible and necessary to build trusting relationships that foster teaching improvement. If your leadership requires some changes and you've committed yourself to growth, you will succeed. There are countless books, classes, and workshops that can be read or attended to help guide your change process. The biggest key is commitment to and belief in your ability to make changes. It's your own growth mindset that will drive you. Think of the mindset modeling you demonstrate by making the change.

With commitment, your efforts will prove successful, but there will be additional implementation challenges because of the differences between your previous actions and the ones you plan to use now. These issues will affect the implementation discussion meeting, and it will take you longer to build teacher trust. For those making changes, you deserve applause. It takes a courageous individual to make changes to one's style of leadership. You are modeling risk taking and vulnerability in taking this action, which is ideal leader action.

So, you've committed to making the change, and you're working on your growth. You know, though, that TBO will be a significantly different style than what your teachers are used to experiencing. At the explanation meeting, how do you deal with the fact that teachers will have their doubts about the model and you because of the past?

The best course of action, after describing the model and its benefits, is honesty. Tell your teachers that you're going to make a change in the way you lead. You're going to be more supportive. You know it will take time to build trusting relationships and demonstrate that you are here to work with teachers. Acknowledge and own past actions. If you haven't observed as much as you are supposed to, own that. If you've been too critical, own it. If you don't really know your teachers and their personalities, strengths, and growth areas, own that. Tell them that your plan is to continually add marbles to the trust jar. Tell them that your hope is that with time, trust will develop and teachers will feel more safe taking risks in practice. Rehumanizing education requires courageous leadership. As you give them a glimpse into that possibility and back it up, they'll hold on to it as their vision, too (Brown 2012).

SUSTAINING SUCCESS

Observation works when leaders, schools, and districts combine strong administrative commitment to evaluation and insistence that it be done right. Without that commitment and insistence, evaluation likely will be eclipsed by other, more apparently urgent responsibilities and demands. Meaningful teacher evaluation will occur only when district leadership insists on it, checks on it, and assigns resources to make it work (Wise et al. 1984). Initial success with TBO matters, but sustained success will matter more.

There are tools and actions that ensure continued success using TBO. Chief among these—and in line with the Rand report finding on teacher evaluation—is a commitment to the model not only from principals and assistant principals but also from those working above them, be they principal supervisors or superintendents. Superintendents and principal supervisors have to understand and appreciate the value TBO brings to improved teaching and learning and in turn make sure that TBO is a continuing focus. This focused support includes training, moderation, and accountability. Superintendents must understand TBO, and it is important that principal supervisors be trained in TBO themselves. Being well trained allows them to support principal growth using the model. Also, district leaders must realize that levels of initial and sustained success will vary by principal. They must encourage and support principals who encounter snags that can accompany implementation, much like they would want principals to do with teachers and much like they would want teachers to do with students.

Principal supervisors can provide accountability and support by engaging in their own observation process with principals and assistant principals. They can accompany school leaders on observations and reflective conversations, observing the observers. They can maintain a regular schedule, just like principals do, thereby modeling good practice and adding an accountability element as well. When principals know they will be periodically accompanied on observations and reflective conversations by their supervisors in a supported manner, it adds extra encouragement. Just as many teachers appreciate that the unannounced visits keep them on top of their game, principal supervisor visits can fulfill the same function by making sure that principals are keeping up with observations and good practice.

When principal supervisors attend observations and reflective conversations, it also allows moderation to take place, ensuring that observers are generally seeing and commenting on the same things. Certainly moderation within a building with all observers doing observations together is also helpful. The same goes for observers from nearby buildings; go to each other's schools and do observations together to make sure you are on the same page.

Weekly in-building observer meetings help the process in many ways. Combining efforts to game-plan best courses of support actions for teachers, holding each other accountable for doing visits, and supporting each other in the process all help sustain TBO success.

In the end, it will be a glorious day when teachers everywhere are being observed frequently, working positively with supportive leaders to take risks and improve teaching and learning. TBO provides a method to create a culture that can accomplish this long-elusive goal: using the observation process to foster meaningful, measurable continuous improvement. It can start with you. Your initiative can start a groundswell of action that causes a transformative positive change in the teaching and learning process around the world. Let's go make it happen.

Bibliography

Australian Society for Evidence Based Teaching. 2020. Productive teacher student relationships affect sttudents' results. http://www.evidencebasedteaching.org.au/crash-course-evidence-based-teaching/teacher-student-relationships.

Balkcom, Stephen. 1992. Cooperative learning. June. https://www2.ed.gov/pubs/OR/Consumer Guides/cooplear.html.

Berger, Ron, Libby Woodfin, and Leah Rugen. 2014. *Leaders of their own learning: Transforming schools through student-engaged assessment.* San Francisco: Jossey-Bass.

Black, Paul, and Dylan Wiliam. 1998. Assessment for learning in the classroom. https://sk.sagepub.com/books/assessment-and-learning-2e/n2.xml.

———. 2005. The formative purpose: Assessment must first promote learning. *Yearbook of the National Society for the Study of Education.* https://www.academia.edu/9737232/The_Formative_Purpose_Assessment_Must_First_Promote_Learning.

Bogdanovich, Patricia. 2014. Higher-order questions. October 28. https://dataworks-ed.com/blog/2014/10/higher-order-questions.

Boser, Ulrich. 2014. *The leap: The science of trust and why it matters.* Boston: New Harvest/Houghton Mifflin Harcourt.

Brown, Brené. 2012. *Daring greatly: How the courage to be vulnerable transforms the way we live, love, parent, and lead.* London: Penguin Life.

Bryk, Anthony S., and Barbara L. Schneider. 2002. *Trust in schools: A core resource for improvement.* New York: Russell Sage Foundation.

Burton, Ella. 2010. High level thinking and questioning strategies. February 23. https://files.eric.ed.gov/fulltext/ED537922.pdf.

Center for Teaching and Learning. 2019. Engaging students in learning. https://www.washington.edu/teaching/topics/engaging-students-in-learning.

Cerbin, Bill, and Brian Kopp. 2004. Performances of understanding—The classroom inquiry cycle: An online tutorial. https://sites.google.com/a/uwlax.edu/sotl/developing-a-research-focus/focusing-on-understanding/performances-of-understanding.

Chappuis, Jan. 2005. Helping students understand assessment. November. http://www.ascd.org/publications/educational-leadership/nov05/vol63/num03/Helping-Students-Understand-Assessment.aspx.

———. 2012. How am I doing? *Educational Leadership.* September. http://www.ascd.org/publications/educational-leadership/sept12/vol70/num01/%C2%A3How-Am-I-Doing%C2%A2
%C2%A3.aspx.

Cogan, Morris L. 1973. *Clinical supervision.* Boston: Houghton Mifflin.

Couros, George. 2015. *The innovator's mindset: Empower learning, unleash talent, and lead a culture of creativity.* San Diego, CA: Dave Burgess Consulting.

Cowan, Nelson. 2014. Working memory underpins cognitive development, learning, and education. *Educational Psychology Review.* June 1. https://www.ncbi.nlm.nih.gov/pmc/articles/PMC4207727.

Dotson, Jeanie M. 2001. Kagan Publishing & Professional Development. *Kagan Online Magazine.* http://www.kaganonline.com/free_articles/research_and_rationale/increase_achieve ment.php.

Dweck, Carol S. 2006. *Mindset: The new psychology of success.* New York: Random House.

Dweck, Carol. 2016. What having a "growth mindset" actually means. *Harvard Business Review.* January 13. https://hbr.org/2016/01/what-having-a-growth-mindset-actually-means.

Dynarski, Mark. 2016. Teacher observations have been a waste of time and money. December 8. https://www.brookings.edu/research/teacher-observations-have-been-a-waste-of-time-and -money.

Ferlazzo, Larry. 2014. Response: Formative assessments are "powerful." *Education Week.* November 30. http://blogs.edweek.org/teachers/classroom_qa_with_larry_ferlazzo/2014/11.

Fleischer, Cathy, Scott Filkins, Antero Garcia, Kathryn Mitchell Pierce, Lisa Scherff, Franki Sibberson, and Millie Davis. 2013. Formative assessment that truly informs instruction. October 21. http://www.ncte.org/library/NCTEFiles/Resources/Positions/formative-assess ment_single.pdf.

Foresi Follow, S. 2013. Learning targets: Delving deeper into the performance of understanding. September 26. https://www.slideshare.net/sforesi/learning-targets-delving-deeper-into-the-performance-of-nderstanding.

Francis, Erik M. 2018. "Activity vs. Inquiry—Which Truly Promotes Cognitive Rigor?" Maverik Education LLC, Scottsdale, AZ. August 26.

———. 2016. *Now that's a good question! How to promote cognitive rigor through classroom questioning.* Alexandria, VA: Association for Supervision and Curriculum Development.

Frey, Nancy, and Douglas Fisher. 2011. *The formative assessment action plan: Practical steps to more successful teaching and learning.* Moorabbin: Hawker Brownlow Education.

Fullan, Michael. 2002. The change leader. May. http://www.ascd.org/publications/educational-leadership/may02/vol59/num08/The-Change-Leader.aspx.

Glasser, William. 1998. *Choice theory: A new psychology of personal freedom.* New York: HarperCollins.

Goldhammer, Robert, Robert Henry Anderson, and Robert J. Krajewski. 1993. *Clinical supervision: Special methods for the supervision of teachers.* Fort Worth, TX: Harcourt Brace Jovanovich College Publishers.

Goleman, Daniel. 1995. *Emotional intelligence: Why it can matter more than IQ.* London: Bloomsbury.

Good, Thomas L., and Jere E. Brophy. 2003. *Looking in classrooms.* London: Allyn & Bacon.

Gordon, Jon. 2017. *The power of positive leadership.* Hoboken, NJ: John Wiley & Sons.

Gottman, John Mordechai, and Nan Silver. 2015. *The seven principles for making marriage work.* New York: Harmony Books.

Greenleaf, Robert K. 2002. *Servant leadership: A journey into the nature of legitimate power and greatness.* New York: Paulist Press.

Guskey, Thomas. 2014. Rethinking classroom observation. May. http://www.ascd.org/publica tions/educational-leadership/may14/vol71/num08/Rethinking-Classroom-Observation.aspx.

Hattie, John. 2008. *Visible learning: A synthesis of over 800 meta-analyses relating to achievement.* Abingdon: Taylor & Francis.

Hess, Rick. 2011. Straight up conversation: Teacher eval guru Charlotte Danielson. *Education Week.* June 23. http://blogs.edweek.org/edweek/rick_hess_straight_up/2011/06/straight_up _conversation_teacher_eval_guru_charlotte_danielson.html.

Institute for Health and Human Potential. 2019. What is emotional intelligence? https://www.ihhp.com/meaning-of-emotional-intelligence.

Intel. 2007. Teacher and peer feedback. http://www.schoolnet.org.za/teach10/resources/dep/feedback/index.htm.

Johnson, David W., and Roger T. Johnson. 2018. What is cooperative learning? April. http://www.co-operation.org/what-is-cooperative-learning.

Kagan, Spencer. 2014. Effect size reveals the impact of Kagan structures and cooperative learning. *Kagan Online Magazine*. https://www.kaganonline.com/free_articles/dr_spencer_kagan/384/Effect-Size-Reveals-the-Impact-of-Kagan-Structures-and-Cooperative-Learning.

———. 2011. Why call on just one when we can call on everyone? *Kagan Online Magazine*. https://www.kaganonline.com/free_articles/dr_spencer_kagan/303/Why-Call-on-Just-One-When-We-Can-Call-on-Everyone.

Kersten, Thomas A., and Marla S. Israel. 2005. Teacher evaluation: Principals' insights and suggestions for improvement. *Planning and Changing* 36, no. 1 and 2: 47–67. https://files.eric.ed.gov/fulltext/EJ737642.pdf.

Killian, Shaun. 2016. 8 strategies Robert Marzano & John Hattie agree on. http://www.evidencebasedteaching.org.au/robert-marzano-vs-john-hattie.

———. 2017. *How to give feedback to students: The advanced guide*. Andergrove: Evidence Based Teaching.

Knight, Jim. Coaching. 2009. https://learningforward.org/wp-content/uploads/2018/03/knight301.pdf.

Knight, Jim, Marti Elford, Michael Hock, Devona Dunakack, Barbara Bradley, Donald D. Deshler, and David Knight. 2015. 3 steps to great coaching. February. https://learningforward.org/journal/february-2015-issue/3-steps-to-great-coaching.

Kosfield, Michael. 2008. Brain trust. September 1. https://greatergood.berkeley.edu/article/item/brain_trust.

Kruse, Kevin. 2016. 15 surprising things productive people do differently. *Forbes Magazine*. January 20. https://www.forbes.com/sites/kevinkruse/2016/01/20/15-surprising-things-productive-people-do-differently/#92466e44b27c.

Marshall, Kim. 2013. *Rethinking teacher supervision and evaluation*, 2nd ed. San Francisco, CA: John Wiley & Sons.

Marzano, Robert J., Jana S. Marzano, and Debra J. Pickering. 2003. *Classroom management that works: Research-based strategies for every teacher*. Alexandria, VA: Association for Supervision and Curriculum Development.

Marzano, Robert J., and Michael D. Toth. 2013. *Teacher evaluation that makes a difference: A new model for teacher growth and student achievement*. Alexandria, VA: Association for Supervision and Curriculum Development.

McCarthy, John. 2017. *So all can learn: A practical guide to differentiation*. Lanham, MD: Rowman & Littlefield.

McGowan, Bryan S. 2015. The relationship between learning and the limitations of our working memory. March 3. http://www.archemedx.com/blog/the-relationship-between-learning-and-the-limitations-of-our-working-memory/#.Wr6rEIjwbD5.

Medina, John. 2014. *Brain rules: 12 principles for surviving and thriving at work, home and school*. Seattle, WA: Pear Press.

Moss, Connie M., and Susan M. Brookhart. 2009. *Advancing formative assessment in every classroom: A guide for instructional leaders*. Alexandria, VA: Association for Supervision and Curriculum Development.

———. 2012. *Learning targets: Helping students aim for understanding in today's lesson*. Alexandria, VA: Association for Supervision and Curriculum Development.

National Education Association. 2001. Research spotlight on cooperative learning. http://www.nea.org/tools/16870.htm.

Neves, Pedro. 2014. How to promote employee risk taking? (People and Society). http://www.novasbe.unl.pt/faculty-research/research-highlights/821.

New South Wales Department of Education. 2015. Types of feedback. http://www.ssgt.nsw.edu.au/documents/1types_feedback.pdf.

O'Leary, Matt. 2014. *Classroom observation: A guide to the effective observation of teaching and learning*. Abingdon: Routledge.

———. 2017. *Reclaiming lesson observation: Supporting excellence in teacher learning*. London: Routledge.

Palmer, Parker J. 2017. *The courage to teach: Exploring the inner landscape of a teacher's life.* San Francisco: Jossey-Bass.

Perkins, David, and Tina Blythe. 1994. Putting understanding up front. February. http://www.ascd.org/publications/educational-leadership/feb94/vol51/num05/Putting-Understanding-Up-Front.aspx.

Popham, James W. 2013. Waving the flag for formative assessment. *Education Week.* January 8. https://www.edweek.org/ew/articles/2013/01/09/15popham.h32.html.

Rock, Marcia L., Madeline Gregg, Edwin Ellis, and Robert A. Gable. 2008. REACH: A framework for differentiating classroom instruction. https://libres.uncg.edu/ir/uncg/f/M_Rock_REACH_2008.pdf.

Rosenberg, Marshall B. 2015. *Nonviolent communication: A language of life.* Encinitas, CA: PuddleDancer Press.

Smith, Dean, John Kilgo, and Sally Jenkins. 2002. *A coach's life:* New York: Random House.

Stecher, Brian M., Deborah J. Holtzman, Michael S. Garet, Laura S. Hamilton, et al. 2018. Impacts of the Intensive Partnerships Initiative. June 21. https://www.rand.org/pubs/research_reports/RR2242.html.

Stiggins, Richard J., and Daniel L. Duke. 1988. *The case for commitment to teacher growth: Research on teacher evaluation.* Albany: State University of New York Press.

Stiggins, Rick. 2004. New assessment for a new school mission. *Phi Delta Kappan* 86, no. 1: 22–27. https://doi.org/10.117/003172170408600106.

Stinson, Janet Lee. 2012. What the heck is an exemplar. June 21. http://weinspirefutures.com/our-community/what-the-heck-is-an-exemplar.

Strickland, Cindy A. 2009. *Professional development for differentiating instruction: An ASCD action tool.* Alexandria, VA: Association for Supervision and Curriculum Development.

Stronge, James H., and Pamela D. Tucker. 2003. *Handbook on teacher evaluation: Assessing and improving performance.* Larchmont, NY: Eye on Education.

Thompson, Ethel. 1952. So begins—so ends the supervisor's day. *Education Leadership.* November. http://www.ascd.org/ASCD/pdf/journals/ed_lead/el_195211_thompson.pdf.

TNTP. 2013. Fixing classroom observations: How common core will change the way we look at teaching. November 12. https://tntp.org/publications/view/evaluation-and-development/fixing-classroom-observations-how-common-core-will-change-teaching.

Tomlinson, Carol Ann. 2014. *The differentiated classroom: Responding to the needs of all learners.* Alexandria, VA: Association for Supervision and Curriculum Development.

———. 2015. Effective differentiation: A guide for teachers and leaders. September 17. https:/files.eric.ed.gov/fulltext/ED562601.pdf.

Tsolaki, Eleni, and Mary Koutselini. 2012. Differentiation of teaching and learning mathematics: An action research study in tertiary education. *International Journal of Mathematical Education in Science and Technology.* August 20. https://www.academia.edu/29123490/Differentiation_of_teaching_and_learning_mathematics_an_action_research_study_in_tertiary_education.

Venuto, Allison. 2015. Exploring new teaching goals: The 10-2-2 strategy. *Delta Kappa Gamma Bulletin* 82, no. 2: 11–12.

Volk, Steven. 2017. Patrik Hultberg: Instructional design and cognitive load theory. April 3. https://glcateachlearn.org/patrik-hultberg-instructional-design-and-cognitive-load-theory.

Wiest, Brianna. 2018. The psychology of daily routine. *Thought Catalog.* October 13. https://thoughtcatalog.com/brianna-wiest/2015/10/the-psychology-of-daily-routine-7-reasons-why-people-who-do-the-same-things-each-day-tend-to-be-happier-than-those-who-chase-adventure.

Wiggins, Grant. 2012. Seven keys to effective feedback. *Educational Leadership.* September. http://www.ascd.org/publications/educational-leadership/sept12/vol70/num01/Seven-Keys-to-Effective-Feedback.aspx.

Winters, Marcus A. 2012. How to grade teachers. https://www.nationalaffairs.com/publications/detail/how-to-grade-teachers.

Wise, Arthur E., Linda Darling-Hammond, Harriet Tyson-Bernstein, and Milbrey Wallin McLaughlin. 2005. The formative purpose: Assessment must first promote learning. *Year-*

book of the National Society for the Study of Education. https://www.academia.edu/9737232/The_Formative_Purpose_Assessment_Must_First_Promote_Learning.

———. 2004. Performances of understanding—The classroom inquiry cycle: An online tutorial. https://sites.google.com/a/uwlax.edu/sotl/developing-a-research-focus/focusing-on-understanding/performances-of-under standing.

———. 1984. *Teacher evaluation: A study of effective practices.* Santa Monica, CA: Rand.

About the Author

Craig Randall received his bachelor's degree (yes, in English) from the University of Washington, his master's in education in guidance and counseling from Saint Martin's University, and his principal certification from Western Washington University.

Craig has worked as an elementary and middle school counselor and has been a collegiate basketball coach. He has been a teacher at the elementary, middle, and high school levels as well as in college. And, of course, he has pursued his passion and calling: being an assistant principal and principal. Craig has worked for schools both in the United States and overseas. Although he didn't know it at the time, these varied work experiences set him up perfectly to develop a model of teacher observation focused on building trusting relationships that spark teaching and learning growth.

Now, as the founder of Trust Based Enterprises, Craig is driven to guide school leaders to successfully adopt and use trust-based observations on a path leading to an unprecedented transformation in the way supervisors observe. His goal is to transform the world of teacher observations, empowering observers to build supportive relationships with their teachers—relationships that foster risk taking, which in turn dramatically improve teaching and learning.

Craig currently lives in the rainy but beautiful Pacific Northwest with the best educator he knows, his wife and new teacher mentor, Michele, and twins who are soon to be high school graduates, Acalia and Craigo.

To learn more about Craig or trust-based observations, go to www.trust based.com. To contact Craig, e-mail him directly at craig@trustbased.com.

Made in the USA
Monee, IL
08 June 2021

70098958R140125